Cambridge Elements

Elements in the Philosophy of Martin Heidegger
edited by
Filippo Casati
Lehigh University
Daniel O. Dahlstrom
Boston University

HEIDEGGER ON PRESENCE

Richard Polt
Xavier University

CAMBRIDGE UNIVERSITY PRESS

Shaftesbury Road, Cambridge CB2 8EA, United Kingdom

One Liberty Plaza, 20th Floor, New York, NY 10006, USA

477 Williamstown Road, Port Melbourne, VIC 3207, Australia

314–321, 3rd Floor, Plot 3, Splendor Forum, Jasola District Centre, New Delhi – 110025, India

103 Penang Road, #05–06/07, Visioncrest Commercial, Singapore 238467

Cambridge University Press is part of Cambridge University Press & Assessment, a department of the University of Cambridge.

We share the University's mission to contribute to society through the pursuit of education, learning and research at the highest international levels of excellence.

www.cambridge.org
Information on this title: www.cambridge.org/9781009550932
DOI: 10.1017/9781009550949

© Richard Polt 2025

This publication is in copyright. Subject to statutory exception and to the provisions of relevant collective licensing agreements, no reproduction of any part may take place without the written permission of Cambridge University Press & Assessment.

When citing this work, please include a reference to the DOI 10.1017/9781009550949

First published 2025

A catalogue record for this publication is available from the British Library

ISBN 978-1-009-55093-2 Hardback
ISBN 978-1-009-55092-5 Paperback
ISSN 2976-5668 (online)
ISSN 2976-565X (print)

Cambridge University Press & Assessment has no responsibility for the persistence or accuracy of URLs for external or third-party internet websites referred to in this publication and does not guarantee that any content on such websites is, or will remain, accurate or appropriate.

Heidegger On Presence

Elements in the Philosophy of Martin Heidegger

DOI: 10.1017/9781009550949
First published online: March 2025

Richard Polt
Xavier University
Author for correspondence: Richard Polt, polt@xavier.edu

Abstract: Heidegger calls the thought that "being is presence" the "thunderbolt" that led him to link being and time and inspired his deconstruction of Western metaphysics. However, the scope of the concept of presence varies in his texts; the narrower it is, the more dramatic yet less plausible is his "thunderbolt." What is presence? Does Heidegger ultimately reject presence as the meaning of being, or does he accept it if conceived broadly enough? This Element surveys the meaning and status of "presence" in Heidegger. It argues that Heidegger maintains a critical perspective, and that his critique can be applied not only to the tradition as interpreted in his "history of being," but also to contemporary phenomena such as information technology.

Keywords: Martin Heidegger, being, presence, ontology, time

© Richard Polt 2025

ISBNs: 9781009550932 (HB), 9781009550925 (PB), 9781009550949 (OC)
ISSNs: 2976-5668 (online), 2976-565X (print)

Contents

Method of Citation   1

1 How Does It Stand with Presence?   2

2 The Meaning of "Being"   7

3 The Meaning of "Presence"   11

4 Heidegger's Developing Thought on Presence   21

5 Presence in the History of Being   37

6 Presence and Engagement   58

References   64

Method of Citation

With few exceptions, references to Heidegger's writings are to *Sein und Zeit*, 11th ed., or to volumes of the *Complete Edition* (*Gesamtausgabe*) of his writings. *Sein und Zeit* is cited as "SZ" followed by a page number (e.g., "SZ: 15"); references to volumes of the *Gesamtausgabe* are cited as "GA" followed by the volume number, the date of composition of the passage cited (if known), and page number (e.g., "GA55, 1943: 19"). All translations are mine. All italics in quotations are original, except when I translate *das Seiende* as "what *is*." Most other English translations include the pagination of the German original, making it possible to dispense with citing the translations' pagination. In the case of exceptions, the German pagination is given followed by a slash and the pagination of the English translation (e.g., "GA9, 1929: 106/84"). When the cited contents of a GA volume are translated in more than one English volume, an acronym of the relevant English title is given. A full list of primary texts and their translations can be found at the beginning of the References section.

1 How Does It Stand with Presence?

"*Being is presence*," writes Heidegger. This "decisive experience of my path of thinking cannot be remembered often enough" (GA98, ca. 1950: 278).

He recalls "the simple, but also barely developed recollection of being as presencing, as which time itself clears itself... It is impossible to say why and how, unmerited and unwanted in any respect, this recollective thought was gifted to the thinking that I sought." This "fundamental experience" was "the sole thunderbolt that struck my thinking existence [*Dasein*] ... The riches of what can be experienced here and what is still reserved for recollection exceed everything that the paths of a thinking could ever discover and bring to light" (GA82, 1943: 354–55).

Thinking being as presence means recovering a legacy and exploring possibilities, engaging in our future and our past. Presence itself – Heidegger's thunderbolt announces – is a present, a gift of time. This thought promises still more to us than it offered to Heidegger himself, despite his decades of meditation.

But in order to pick up the trail where he left it, we must better understand this lightning that struck him in the early 1920s and provoked him until the end. On its own, the assertion that "being is presence" leaves many matters in the dark.

First, what does "being" mean? A century after *Being and Time*, Heidegger's most dedicated interpreters still disagree.

What does "presence" mean? How narrowly should it be taken?

What is the meaning of the "is" in "being is presence"? Is it phenomenological, describing experience? Historical, characterizing the tradition? Or does this distinction break down in Heidegger's thought?

Is being *necessarily* presence? Or is this contingent? Or both: a contingent necessity for the Westernized world, our destiny? If so, how does presence shape Western metaphysics?

Are there alternatives to presence? If so, is Heidegger seeking them? Does he want to expand the sense of being beyond presence – or even leave presence behind? Some readers are convinced that he is critiquing presence, while others think he cherishes presence in its richest form.

Although his insight into being as presence was a "decisive experience," is it the heart of his thought? Or a provocation that led him to more fundamental issues?

Beyond the daunting challenge of understanding Heidegger, there is the question of whether he is right. Is being *truly* presence? Just how illuminating is this thought – phenomenologically and historically?

Finally, above these questions hovers the question of what difference they make. Are they academic issues, of interest only to specialists? Or – Heidegger is sure of this – do they spell the fate of our planet? He claims that not just philosophy but our dominant ways of handling and judging all that *is* rely on an unrecognized experience of being as presence – so we are blind to the source and limits of our ways of illuminating things. Is this so?

We cannot answer any of these questions in isolation; they rebound on each other. If we are already plunged into the history of being as presence, it would be too crude to define presence phenomenologically, and then turn to the history of philosophy. Phenomenology without history is naive, while history of philosophy without phenomenology is mere doxography.

The questions concerning presence hang together. To recall this entire problematic, we can use a vague Heideggerian locution: "How does it stand with presence?" (GA78, 1942: 169).

The problematic is compounded by Heidegger's shifting thoughts and usages. These shifts are not mere confusion, but a journey along a "path." Some seeming inconsistencies can also be explained by different contexts. In particular, when we are in the midst of his sympathetic interpretations of the tradition, especially early Greek thought, his own critical standpoint can become invisible.

Still, some discrepancies pose obstacles to our investigation. Above all, Heidegger describes "presence" narrowly and broadly. The narrower it becomes, the more provocative the claim "being is presence" – but also the less plausible.

The narrowest sense of presence would be bounded, uniform, necessary being, disclosed without remainder in an eternal "now." Parmenides' Fragment 8, lines 5–6, offer a classic formula for this vision: οὐδέ ποτ' ἦν οὐδ' ἔσται, ἐπεὶ νῦν ἔστιν ὁμοῦ πᾶν, / ἕν, συνεχές. "Neither was it nor will it be, for it is now, all together, one, continuous." Here Parmenides – as usually read – binds what *is* to its presence in the present: immutable immediacy, standing noonday. "Everything purely full, no emptiness, no 'away,' no absence in being as such, but only presence . . . simple collectedness in the present" (GA35, 1932: 167–68). We can call this the *Eleatic* sense of presence.

If this is what "presence" means, the *phenomenological* claim "being is presence" seems obviously false. The Eleatic vision expressly *rejects* the phenomena. What appears to sensation contradicts logic and must be denied, as Zeno tries to show with his paradoxes. Heidegger, we will see, complicates this issue with an unconventional reading of Parmenides as describing a *horizon* of presence within which surface phenomena appear (GA35: 176). But inevitably, the more narrowly one means that "being is presence," the more one excludes from being.

As a *historical* claim, "being is presence" in the Eleatic sense would be provocative, aggressive – and again – seemingly false. One can even doubt whether Parmenides himself embraced the view he ascribed to a goddess (Adluri, 2011). And surely, very few later thinkers unreservedly join the Eleatic rejection of all so-called nonbeing. The atomists claim nonbeing *is* as void. Plato's *Sophist* defends nonbeing as difference. Aristotle defends nonbeing as potency and change. Descartes and Leibniz discover the mathematical logic of motion. Nietzsche shudders at "the inert stable dead being of Parmenides" (1962: 92), "un-Greek as no other" (1962: 69), and celebrates "the innocence of becoming" (1997: 36–37).

The broadest sense of presence would include all these non-Eleatic phenomena: emptiness, otherness, multiplicity, potential, change. All are "present": they show up, they make a difference to us. Otherwise we couldn't even refer to them. Absence itself can be vividly present (just consider the question, "Where's my phone?").

Now "being is presence" is far more flexible and plausible – so plausible that it is trivial. How could this triviality be a "decisive experience"? What would be the impact of such a feeble "thunderbolt"?

If neither extreme is right, perhaps we need a concept of presence that packs a punch *and* lands a blow: a provocative, questionable, but defensible claim that has both historical and phenomenological resonance.

Or maybe the punch of Heidegger's thought does not lie in presence, but in what makes presence possible: in his earlier work, time; later, appropriation (*Ereignis*). Of course, these words are no less in need of interpretation than "being" and "presence." And there are more puzzles: Are time and appropriation *phenomena*? If so, aren't they present in some sense, so that presence rather than they would be most fundamental? If not, how can we think of them at all?

Those of us trying to think through these issues in English face further obstacles. Some thirty expressions in Heidegger can be translated with variations on "presence," "présent," or "présent." Which word is he using, and does it make a difference?

Heidegger's vocabulary obviously did not follow a set of rigid definitions for half a century. However, translations should let Anglophone readers recognize which German word he uses. Since we are considering developmental questions, it also helps to know when a passage was composed. To that end, I indicate years of composition, whenever they can be ascertained; all translations are mine; and I translate Heidegger's words for presence as follows. Inevitably, some of these choices are arbitrary. I will occasionally insert the German as a reminder or clarification.

An-wesen	presence-to
An-wesung	pre-sencing
Anwesen	presence
anwesen	to presence
anwesend	present (adj.)
Anwesende, das	what is present
Anwesenden, die	those that presence
Anwesendes	what presences
Anwesendmachen	present-making
Anwesendsein	being-present
Anwesenheit	presentness
Anwesung	presencing
entgegen-warten	presently await-toward
entgegenwarten	presently await
Gegen-wart	awaiting-toward
Gegenwart	the present
gegenwärtig (adj.)	in the present
gegenwärtig (adv.)	presently
Gegenwärtige, das	what is in the present
gegenwärtigen	make present
Gegenwärtigkeit	in-the-present-ness
Gegenwärtigsein	being-in-the-present
Gegenwärtigung	making-present
Mitanwesenheit	copresentness
präsent	Present
Präsentation	presentation
präsentieren	to present
präsentisch	present-oriented
Präsenz, Praesenz	Presence
ungegenwärtigen	to unpresent
vergegenwärtigen	presentify
Vergegenwärtigung	presentification

To further confuse matters, certain expressions in Heideggerian English appear to refer directly to presence but do not. "Presence-at-hand" and "objective presence" are not misguided translations of *Vorhandenheit*, but the German word does not explicitly name presence. As for *vorstellen*, I follow the tradition of translating it as "represent," but it literally means "to set before."

More problematically, the verb *wesen* has been translated as "to presence." *Das Seyn west* becomes "beyng presences." "Beyng" is a convenient counterpart to the antique *Seyn* – but is *wesen* equivalent to *anwesen*? "*Anwesung* constitutes the first flaring up of *one Wesung* of beyng" (GA65, 1936–38: 31). "Now the essence of beyng no longer means only *Anwesenheit*, but the full *Wesung* of ... truth" (GA65: 32). "*Wesung*, not grasped as such, is *Anwesung*" (GA65: 189). We must avoid translating *Wesung* as "presencing"; otherwise, these statements make no sense.

Here is how I translate a few words that are related to presence, but do not directly include it.

Ab-wesen	being absent
Abwesen	absence
abwesen	be absent
abwesend	absent
Abwesenheit	absentness
Ab-wesung	ab-sencing
Abwesung	absencing
gewärtigen	await
vorhanden	at hand
Vorhandenheit	at-handness
Vorhandensein	being-at-hand
vorstellen	represent
Vorstellung	representation
Wesen	essence
wesen	to essence
Wesung	essencing

The varieties of presence have long been a theme for phenomenologists. For example, Husserl analyzes presentification in his 1905 lectures on time-consciousness (1964: 57–71, 116–17, 124–26), edited and cited by Heidegger in 1928 (GA26: 263–64). Other readers have also tackled the sense and status of presence in Heidegger (e.g., Marx, 1971; Carman, 1995; Olafson, 1996; Dastur, 2014; Backman, 2015; Backman et al., 2019). It is beyond my scope to do justice to this intricate literature, although I cite some highlights.

Instead, I focus on Heidegger's own texts – now available in the hundred-some volumes of his *Gesamtausgabe*. I have chosen some striking passages and followed a few important lines of thought. I cannot explain every context, and I encourage readers to explore alternatives. This short study is a set of indications for further research – not a doctrine from either Heidegger or me.

What follows is primarily a study in the history of philosophy. But since history and phenomenology are intertwined, I include a few scenarios that describe experiences and begin experimental reflections, illustrating a few complexities of presence.

Now we must ask: What is being (Section 2)? What is presence, and how broad is its scope (Section 3)? How does Heidegger's critique of presence evolve (Section 4)? How does it apply to the "history of being" (Section 5)? What difference do his thoughts on presence make (Section 6)?

2 The Meaning of "Being"

> *I pry into my memory and discover myself as a prying boy, lifting a slate flagstone in my garden. I almost drop it as the writhing and teeming hits me. Life thrives underneath: a salamander, worms, pillbugs, ants. They must be as shocked by the light as I am by their existence. I savor the shiver that runs through me as I recognize that they're there, that they were already there, and that countless other creatures are squirming under other flagstones on which I've run day after day, never thinking to look beneath.*
> *It's as if I never knew my garden until now.*
> *It's as if I never knew myself until now.*

What does "being" mean? This basic question is still not discussed enough in Heidegger scholarship. "Basic" does not mean easy, and by avoiding it we end up speaking at cross purposes, or not even knowing what we mean. Is Heidegger inquiring into the usage of the word *Sein*? Processes in the universe? Human culture and practice? Or all these and more, without alerting us to the ambiguities?

Being has many aspects. The problem of their unity first stimulated Heidegger's thinking (GA14, 1963: 93/74). Importantly, being embraces essence and existence – "what-being" and "that-being." What it means *that an entity is* is tied to *what kind of entity it is*. "Actuality itself essentially varies ... The full essence of an entity concerns both the *what* of an entity and the *how* of its possible or actual actuality" (GA33, 1931: 223). Existence for a rock is not existence for a salamander. Heidegger's question of being always has this "existential" element, which we obscure if we take him to be asking only about typologies. Although he is not raising "ontic" questions about what in particular is or is not actual, he *is* investigating what it *means* for things to be actual.

This question of meaning is crucial. Being means something to us – we understand it – even though we have trouble articulating it. This understanding conditions every experience, although it usually stays in the background (SZ: 6). As I step on a rock, I understand that its being is rocklike, and that I cannot step on a person as if on a rock. (People do step on each other, but cruelty, inconsideration, and cheerleading are relations to humans, not rocks.)

The being of an entity, then, is what it means *to us* that the entity is, as the kind of entity that it is. Heidegger goes farther: Being is not given at all except to humans as Dasein – the entity who *is the there*, who exists as an opening for encounters with entities. A rock is an entity in itself, a real, independent thing; but in-itselfness, independence, and realness are meanings of being, in effect only for Dasein (SZ: 211–12).

There is good evidence that this correlation endures in Heidegger's thought. "When we say 'beyng,' rightly understood, we say Dasein along with it; and vice versa" (GA82, 1947: 258). "What I call … 'being' requires humanity; being is not being unless humanity is required for its revelation, preservation, and formation" (GA16, 1966: 672/SI 326). "The fundamental thought of my thinking is precisely that being, or the openness of being, *requires* human beings and that, in turn, human beings are human only insofar as they stand in the openness of being" (GA16, 1969: 704/MHC 82).

Accordingly, Thomas Sheehan argues that Heidegger's "being" is intelligibility – what things mean to us as phenomena. Heidegger remains a phenomenologist, and his inquiry remains within finite human existence (2014: 23). But Richard Capobianco counters that Heidegger's later work transcends phenomenology to appreciate the "shimmering unfolding" (2022) of what *is*, its emergence independently of us. He cites passages such as this: "At times, being needs the human essence, but it never depends on existing [*seienden*] humanity. Humanity as historical, as knowing and preserving beings as such, does stand in relation to being; but the claim of the human essence on being itself is not always brought about [*ereignet*] by being itself" (GA6.2, 1941: 441/76). Capobianco comments: "The unending temporal self-showing and shining-forth of Being as *physis* as *aletheia* is not in need of the human being in the strict sense, yet we may say that the human being is 'needed' only as a mirror reflecting back in language the inexhaustible resplendence of Being's manifestation" (2022: 34).

But if being endures on its own, why would it ever require mirroring? And is Heidegger's appreciative interpretation of *physis* his *own* conception of being? His references to being's "independence" emphasize that it is not a human product, but it does not follow that it can occur without us. Being "is *not* at all human in the sense that being could simply be a construct and creation of human representation"; but it "is human in the sense that [it] demands that the human essence preserve [its] truth" (GA80.2, 1950: 973).

A related problem is whether any understanding of being can be truer than another. None can be verified as "correct" by ontic facts, and all are disclosive. But interpretations can "force an entity into concepts that the entity opposes in its way of being" (SZ: 150). For instance, later Heidegger sees cybernetic interpretations of humanity as reductive distortions (GA89, 1964: 685/20; GA89, 1965: 834/123). We always have access to entities; no access is absolute;

but some clearings are richer and deeper – and even within a shallow clearing, we can find hints of depth that let us criticize the predominant understanding.

In sum: Most *entities* do not need us, but *being* requires Dasein. At crucial moments, we are especially challenged to wrestle with being, and we may encounter entities more fully. An entity's "own" way of being is a rich, distinctive way in which it shows up if our understanding of being is broad and flexible enough to let it do so; but there is no showing without Dasein.

We must add a troubling qualification: Sometimes Heidegger sees Dasein as a way of existing that not all people attain. "*Not all humans who are actual – who actually have been or will be – 'exist,' have existed, or will exist, in the sense* in which we understand existence" (GA35, 1932: 84). "*Being* the there is a basic *possibility* of being human. The beyng of the there does not happen everywhere and at every time where humans are" (GA80.2, 1936: 669). This thought invites arrogant biases, and Heidegger is more persuasive when he presents Dasein as the universally human way of being, albeit one that we rarely recognize and embrace.

With these points in mind, I think Sheehan's equation of being with meaning works well. All entities show up as significant: "Even the most trivial is meaningful – just trivially so. Even the most worthless is meaningful" (GA58, 1919–20: 104). Entities appear thanks to established ways for them to mean something to us; and they have no meaning unless there is someone for whom they are meaningful. We should add that some meanings are more disclosive than others; that meaning shifts; that it is threatened by meaninglessness; and that Heidegger's "question of being" also concerns what exceeds meaning, including the mysterious origination of meaning itself (Polt, 2011). We should also remember that even though there is no meaning apart from Dasein, we do not make meaning from scratch. It happens *for* us. Then we may develop or challenge it.

I also find it helpful to think of being as the difference it makes that there is something instead of nothing. This phrase emphasizes "that-being," but not exclusively, since *that* something is embodies *what* it is: The essence of a salamander or a symphony implies its own way of being something instead of nothing. Again, this makes a difference only *to someone*, but we do not *create* the difference. My phrase is not a definition of being, only a circumlocution: The locution is circular, since it uses the word *is* to express *being*. But this is an advantage: It keeps the meaning of being empty, so that we can genuinely ask *what* being means.

The difference an entity makes is all-important to how we experience it, think of it, and behave toward it. What we accept as being we consider relevant. What counts as nonbeing we ignore as nugatory. The question of being matters because it is all about "mattering" (Pippin, 2024: 31). Show me what being means to you, and I'll show you who you are.

One more ambiguity has to be addressed. Heidegger's *Sein* often refers to "the being of beings" or "beingness" – what it means in general for what *is* to *be*. But especially when he favors the obsolete spelling *Seyn*, it is "the ground in which all that *is* first comes as such to its truth" (GA65, 1936–38: 76–77). "Beyng essences as the *event [Ereignis] of the grounding of the there*" (GA65: 183). This can be understood as the *emergence* of beingness. It is not meaning, but the *donation* of meaning.

In which sense did Heidegger mean that "being is presence"? Usually, it is clearly the first sense. "What *is* is what presences in its presentness" (GA91, 1932: 252): Presence is what it means for beings to be. But there are some contexts, especially when he speaks of "presencing," where he seems to mean an event of emergence, and we might suspect it is the emergence of beingness.

We will return in due course to presencing. But for now, and at least in most contexts, "being is presence" says that something is meaningful and makes a difference to us if and only if we accept it as *present*.

This may look tautological. Then, "'what presences' is just another name for beings" (Young, 2002: 10). But in that case, Heidegger's "thunderbolt" would be obvious – and he insists that "being is presence" is anything but that. "Someday one will translate *einai* as 'presence,' or at least think of 'to be' in this sense. One will tacitly come to act as if nothing had happened, as if this other way of saying the word were a lexical trifle instead of the turn in the destiny of being" (GA98, ca. 1950: 163).

> It's now a commonplace that "being" means presence. One even believes that one always meant it in this sense. But this shows that presence has nowhere been properly thought *as the basic characteristic* of being ... Why would it have been necessary [for me] to dedicate all [my] reflections to this one point and to think of the "temporal" character of being qua presence? Being and essence "mean presence, obviously." – Obviously? I don't think so! ... One has never thought [being] as presence ... Otherwise, "being and time" would be *the* ultimate triviality of all philosophy. (GA98: 232–33)

"Being is presence" is supposed to be provocative – so "being" and "presence" cannot be synonyms. "Presence" provides content to a word, "being," that would otherwise be "a fleetingly used name covering up arbitrary, vague representations of something indefinitely general" (GA5, 1946: 349). "'What presences' – describing, for example, an island, that island off in the distance. Mountain – tree – houses – ships – the same goes for 'being' [*'Seiend'*] ... But 'what presences' – speaks more clearly. How so?" (GA73.2: 1230).

Our response requires phenomenology, attention to how beings appear as present and what enables them to do so. But this project is also historical: We have to retrieve the inceptive Greek experience of being as presence.

> If we ever manage to think what is named in the word "presence" in its entire fullness and breadth, which flowered in the Greek experience of the world, then and only then may we instead of "presence" also say: *being*. Without the heartfelt, full, and thought-out remembrance of the destiny of being on the basis of the Greek world, the word "being" remains an empty sound, a hollow shell, or the name for a confused representation. (GA79, 1957: 148)

3 The Meaning of "Presence"

> *A droplet hits the page I'm reading. I look up from my bench at the gray sky, then back to the wet circle on the paper. I watch the circle, keeping it in focus, centering it in my vision. Nothing is hidden: its shape is evident to my eyes and mind. A unit: a point made perceptible, there for me in all clarity. I watch until it fades and evaporates, leaving a faint warp.*
>
> *It was an interlude of sheer beholding – I was absorbed in absorbing the object. Where is that interlude now? Nowhere. Or does it exist in its own way, lodged in the past? Could the moment be established in a circle of its own as a focus of time? Like a word on this page, the moment is there, imprinted durably – or beyond duration. Just as the word is not diminished by surrounding words, other moments do not detract from this one, despite their seeming flow. It need not be swallowed by what appears to follow it; it may even be the point around which other moments orbit.*
>
> *Every moment of true presence is eternal.*

We turn now to Heidegger's accounts of presence, some phenomenological, others historical. Again, these two approaches cannot ultimately be teased apart: Every phenomenon has a heritage, and in turn, our heritage remains opaque unless we try to rediscover the experiences that motivated the tradition.

Our first question concerns the breadth of Heidegger's concept of presence. Does it exclude phenomena such as "readiness-to-hand" (Noë, 2012: 8) or "non-present temporal dimensions" (Kirkland, 2023: 13)? Heidegger's texts can support both "yes" and "no" answers. As an initial approach to his thought on presence, we can collect these passages – first the narrower accounts, then the broader ones.

3.1 Narrow Presence

Heidegger's narrower accounts of presence qualify it, above all, as *beständig* – constant, enduring.

At an extreme, enduring presence is eternity – the Eleatic standing "now." "For the Greeks, being means being-present [*Anwesendsein*], being-in-the-present

[*Gegenwärtigsein*]. This is why what is always in the now is what really *is* and the *archē*, the origin, of all other beings. Every determination of a being ... is derived from something that always is, and understood in terms of it" (GA19, 1924: 34). "What is meant by *ousia* is nothing but *constant presentness* ... The Greeks address something as an entity in the genuine sense when it *satisfies* this understanding of being: constant presentness, what is *always at hand*" (GA31, 1930: 52).

Constancy presents itself as peak presencing; it fulfills an essential impulse in presence. "The presencing of the constant has in itself the relation and tendency to stabilization. And stabilization, seen this way, evidently first reaches its essence in constancy, in an enduring stability that is fixed in itself. This lasting stability would then be what first delimits the essence of presencing" (GA51, 1941: 112).

Note the subjunctive in Heidegger's last statement, which prepares the way for a reversal: "Being is presencing, but not necessarily stabilization in the sense of hardening into stability" (GA51: 113). We will return to the richer sense of presencing; for now, it is enough to see that Eleatic presence is eminently contestable. "Is that then so obvious, that being is understood as constant presence, and do we have to accept this obvious understanding simply because the entirety of Western metaphysics has insisted on this obvious point without worrying about it? Or may and must we ask: What is happening when being is so readily understood as constancy and presence?" (GA31, 1930: 114). "With what right does one assert that 'being' that has no 'not' in it, not passing away, not becoming – the 'eternal' – is pure being? Why should the 'not' be banished from being? Why this dictate? And why is being = constant presentness?" (GA91, 1932: 259). Constancy "arrogates to itself, without meeting any resistance, the determination and guidance of all ways of being and their modifications (e.g. 'modalities')" (GA66, 1938–39: 90). The possible and the actual are subordinated to the necessary, which endures unshakably. Heidegger urges us to resist.

Heidegger sometimes highlights other features of presence in a narrow sense. According to this passage, what is present seems identical with what *is* because showing crowds out the inapparent: Concealment itself gets concealed. "Why does only disclosure disclose itself at first, and only as what is disclosed – in such a way that the disclosed, as soon as it shines and glows, grants what is *present* as such the essence of being that which is?" (GA76, ca. 1936: 8). What is present is available, accessible.

For the Greeks, presence and constancy also involve definiteness. "What is in being is what is shaped in limitation and is thus present and constant in such presence. *Being: formed, stable presence*" (GA36/37, 1933–34: 93). The

Greeks "call form, as opposed to formlessness, what is. For them, what *is* is what delimits itself, as against the limitless and evanescent" (GA45, 1937–38: 136–37).

A different, but no less narrow interpretation of presence takes it as athandness (*Vorhandenheit*). "The beings within the environment that are *already* present are the ones we designate as *at hand*, in contrast to the ready-to-hand. One will perhaps say that precisely this entity at hand – *environmental nature* – is what is most real, the authentic reality of the world ... the primary worldly Presence [*Präsenz*] [is then] the reality of nature" (GA20, 1925: 270–71). What is at hand does not have to be permanent, but it precedes our activities and is independent of them. We tend to take this as what "really" constitutes the world: "the vulgar understanding of being understands 'being' indifferently as athandness" (SZ: 389).

Finally, and crucially, what is present appears in the temporal present (*Gegenwart*). Past and future are then defective presence, no longer or not yet present. "How does the present have this privilege? Don't past and future have just as much right? Doesn't being have to be grasped on the basis of the entirety of temporality?" (GA22, 1926: 314).

If past and future are absent, we must say that "being absent is richer, more powerful, and has a more original essential force than the exaggerated presence. Absence as essentially having-been [*Ge-wesenheit*] and as future. Both as the original splitting of essence and of essencing unity. And finally, presence [is] just a forgetting of this unity" (GA94, ca. 1932: 81).

Since Dasein essentially extends into past and future, its unity must be a temporal gathering rather than a present simultaneity: "Da-sein can never keep itself in *presence* and, as it were, pull itself together into a point. It essences only as *collected*" (GA82, 1936: 84).

Our evidence so far assigns "presence" a tight scope: What is present is a circumscribed object at hand, appearing now, durably or even eternally. "Being is presence" is then a polemical description of the tradition, and Heidegger's line of attack is strong and clear. But is it plausible? The narrower his concept of presence gets, the less convincing is his historical claim. So far, it would seem he simply disregards all attempts in Western metaphysics to overcome Eleatic being. It sounds as if he were – unwittingly – just one among many thinkers who have combated the priority of permanent substance, including Nietzsche, Bergson, and Whitehead.

However, a case can be made that although most Western conceptions of being are irreducible to narrow presence, and even fight it, they still end up taking it as the ideal of full being, whether they admit this or not. It may be that seemingly anti-Eleatic thinkers have, despite themselves, appealed to constancy in a more subtle way.

14   *The Philosophy of Martin Heidegger*

The atomists affirm void, but their atoms are still indestructible substances.

Plato accepts otherness, "the presentness of what is not" (GA19, 1924–25: 193), but is fascinated by the eternal forms as what "beingfully is."

Aristotle admits potency, but gives actuality the upper hand (*Met.* IX.8), and his supreme being is immutable, pure actuality (*Met.* XII.6).

Nietzsche celebrates becoming and power, but (in Heidegger's reading) he eternalizes becoming and absolutizes power, ending in yet another metaphysics.

In our technological age, beings are no longer durable objects but manipulable resources. But even this, one could argue, is a variant of narrow presence: Resources are held steady, ready to be plugged into the system, supplying a *constant* stream of energy and effectiveness.

We will return to the relevance of Heidegger's critique to our own times. First, let's consider some passages that take presence more broadly.

3.2 Broad Presence

Heidegger's narrower accounts of presence coexist with far more generous ones. These passages may suggest that his goal is not to overthrow presence, but to establish a richer sense of it, perhaps by recovering the original experience of "presencing" (*Anwesung*). His enemy may not be presence at all, but its over-narrow interpretation, and the statement "being is presence" may be more phenomenological than historically critical, if it leads us to a sufficiently broad description.

First, there are varieties of presence. "Presence differs according to the character of the entity that is supposed to be present" (GA33, 1931: 182). "Not everything that *is* in some way is present in the same way" (GA8, 1952: 239/236). "Being as presentness can show itself in various ways of Presence" (GA9, 1964: 78).

If being means presence, the greatest threat to being is "the coming of absentness, being-away, the away-ness of what is" (GA34, 1931–32: 140). So a particularly dramatic, even paradoxical, way to broaden the sense of presence is to include absence. Heidegger does so in a number of texts, and also finds this extended presence in Greek philosophy. Notes for his 1924 lectures on Aristotle include absence as a mode of presence (GA18: 376) along with potentiality (380, 393) and movement (380, 387–88). A later reading of Aristotle does the same for privation: In a phenomenon such as cold, "something shows itself, presences, that we thus 'feel'; but in what is presencing and is felt, something is also absencing in such a way that, precisely by virtue of the absencing, we especially feel what is thus present" (GA9, 1939: 296/226). Likewise, if we notice "the bicycle is gone," we experience "not just absentness, but a *presencing* in which *absencing itself* – not what is absent – presences" (GA9: 296–97/226–27). Absence is "an *unpresenting [ungegenwärtigen]* as a definite mode of the present," occuring within "a *definitely modified horizon of the present, of Presence*" (GA24, 1927: 441–42).

There is an obscurity here that concerns negativity itself; Heidegger conjectures that "the essence of the not, nullity, can be interpreted only on the basis of the essence of time" (GA24, 1927: 443). Perhaps temporality itself is pervaded by absence – "*ab-sencing* not as the simple negation of pre-sencing, but the full unfolding of the moment" (GA73.1, ca. late 1930s: 319).

How can absence be a kind of presence? In 1927 Heidegger takes both as modes of a broader phenomenon, *Praesenz* – the horizonal schema opened by the ecstasis of the temporal present. Within this horizon, both absence and presence make sense (GA24: 433, 436). But why call it *Praesenz*, if it embraces both presentness and absentness?

Heidegger addresses this question in 1930, in a historical register. For the Greeks, presence and absence, *parousia* and *apousia*, are not merely variants of some *ousia* that transcends the distinction; *ousia* itself is a more primordial presence (GA31: 61). I will consider this argument in Section 5.2, along with Heidegger's reading of Anaximander, with its claim that "even the absent is present" (GA5, 1946: 347).

Greek poetry also includes absence in presence. In *Antigone*, uncanniness is "presencing in the form of an absencing" (GA53, 1942: 92). Pindar's saying that man is the dream of a shadow takes dreams as a disappearance that itself appears. The shades of the dead, too, have a distinctive presence-of-absence (GA52, 1941–42: 117). Presence and absence also characterize the gods in their nearness and distance (GA73.1: 319). Their "absencing lets us miss presencing and in this way makes us attentive to presence, in which arising and revealing are concealed" (GA75, 1943: 39).

But Heidegger does not try to make his position on presence and absence depend purely on readings of the ancients. Let's turn to some phenomenological claims. "Being is presence, nonbeing absence; but even the absent can be! Absence is multiple, and so is presence, depending in each case on the breadth of ecstatic temporality" (GA34, 1932: 295n).

> What do we mean by present and absent? . . . Here [*da*] and away! Where is here? Here before our eyes; here at hand, where we can just reach out and grab something, what lies in our immediate reach. But how far does this reach extend? . . . Where is the boundary between what is still here and what is already away? My hat, say, is not at hand here, it's away – in another room, maybe. It's away from here, but it's over there in the university . . . What is far away may be "here" on the telephone or radio. Evidently there is *no fixed*

> *boundary* between here and away, everything is both ... *depending on –
> what*? What is not immediately accessible to our senses, what is away, is
> nevertheless here for immediate presentification [*Vergegenwärtigung*], such
> as the Black Forest, the North Sea, Berlin ... Is there anything absent at all,
> then, if we take the sphere of what is present so broadly, and even more
> broadly, so that everything is at hand at once? If there is something absent ...
> then *it can be absent only in a sphere of presentness*. (GA35, 1932: 176)

Heidegger adds: "And that is what Parmenides wants to say!" (GA35: 176). Maybe Parmenides is not as narrow as he seems. In this creative reading, to assert that being "neither was nor will it be, for it is now" is not to claim that what *is* is changeless, but that beings both changing and unchanging, both near and distant, present themselves within presence as the sense of being. Within this sphere, we can "presentify" all that is. We will return to this concept.

Heidegger declares: "all presencing is also in itself absencing. What is present as such – not just subsequently and incidentally, but according to its essence – extends into absence" (GA52, 1941–42: 117). But is this a limitation on presence, an embrace of a broad sense of presence, or a critique of the hegemony of presence, which absorbs even absence? His statements are often open to very different readings. For instance: "The reach of presence shows itself to us in the most pressing way when we consider that even and precisely absence remains determined by a presence, sometimes intensified to the point of uncanniness" (GA14, 1962: 11/7). Is he simply saying that we ought to notice that even the absent is present, as a phenomenological fact? Or is he suggesting there is something oppressive and strange in how presence envelops all experience?

What else is included in presence, broadly conceived?

Presence exceeds the now. What is "not yet presencing, but coming [is] a distinctive kind of Presence ... something not yet at hand but drawing near" (GA20, 1925: 395). "What is no longer in the temporal present is immediately presencing in its absence, as what has been and concerns us" – so "not all presence is necessarily the present" (GA14, 1962: 17–18/13). We can grasp "'having-been' not as a mere shadow of what is in the present, but as a presence-already, as a full mode of presentness, just as much presentness as the present" (GA89, 1963: 666/181).

Again, there is more than one way to take these statements. Is he acknowledging the presence of the future and the past? Or hinting that approaching all time in terms of presence misses the genuine future and past? Our assertoric thought highlights what is at hand and present. But "assertions do not just restrict themselves to what is now in the present, but also refer to what has been and what will be" (GA29/30, 1930: 464). Do we reduce time to presence in our way of speaking and thinking?

If past and future are present, so is becoming. Heidegger credits Aristotle with the thought that becoming is a "change in presence" (GA65, 1936–38: 193) and that "movement belongs to presence itself" (GA83, 1951: 484).

In order to include becoming in presence, he sometimes favors the word *Anwesung* over *Anwesen* or *Anwesenheit*.

> We will attempt to clarify what is most proper to [the Greek concept of being] in a word by saying "presencing" instead of "presentness." What we mean is not mere at-handness, nor in general what exhausts itself in constancy, but presencing in the sense of coming forth into the unconcealed, placing itself in the open. Mere enduring does not capture presencing. (GA9, 1939: 272/208)

"Presencing-to [*An-wesung*] is distinguished by *genesis*, coming forth. Mere presence in the sense of at-handness has already set limits to presencing, coming forth, and so has given up presencing" (GA51, 1941: 113). "'Presentness' is presencing that has been fixed, interrupted, broken, laid out into sections and limits" (GA73.1: 55).

But Heidegger also frequently uses *Anwesen* and *Anwesenheit* in a sense that includes becoming. In 1924 he interprets *kinēsis* as "a particular *presentness*" (GA18: 387). In 1965 he writes, "What we ambiguously and confusingly enough call 'what is' was experienced by the Greek philosophers as what is present ... In presentness they also thought the transition from presence to absence, arriving and vanishing, arising and passing away – that is, movement" (GA16: 624/QCD 216).

Clearly, to insist on the being of becoming is not necessarily to depart from being as presence in a broad but still traditional sense. In fact, the priority of becoming is one metaphysical position among others, with its own line of defenders. Nietzsche is prominent among them, with his view that, as Heidegger puts it, "being as the constant does not correspond to genuine actuality as what flows and transforms itself" (GA46, 1939: 344). Heidegger sees Nietzsche as anticipating twentieth-century technology or "machination," where the churning will to power takes the form of a managed flux of resources. None of this escapes the tradition of being as presence – and even permanence. "The highest form of constancy and presencing is sought in 'becoming'; it initially appears to be the opposite of being and its exclusion, but in truth it seeks the constancy of the ever different, and still wants to rescue change and disappearance into being" (GA66, 1938–39: 92). A constant flow is still constant. To say that "being is becoming does not deny being. To the contrary, the preordained fulfillment of its inceptive essence (*physis – idea – ousia*) is achieved ... through beingness as machination" (GA66: 26). "Nietzsche wants becoming precisely, and above all, *as what endures* – as what properly 'is,' in the sense of the Greek thinkers" (GA47, 1939: 271). He wants perpetuity, even as perpetual overcoming (GA66: 111).

These passages are unmistakably polemical (I set aside the question of whether they are fair). Heidegger shares Nietzsche's animus against frozen eternity, but if he were only affirming becoming, he would just be a Nietzschean. Instead, he wants to identify presence as the root of the being/becoming dichotomy that has haunted metaphysics since its beginning in the experience of *physis*.

> The ambiguity of "being" as constancy in the sense of what is fixed and constancy as the presencing of becoming is grounded on the undeveloped *unambiguity* of "being" as constant presentness, in which the "truth" of *physis* is interpreted according to a particular "temporal" conception that goes unrecognized. The ambiguity with which *Nietzsche* uses the word *being* is thus only the unresolved reflection of *how* all metaphysics thinks and must think its fundamental word ... Nietzsche himself is mixed up in the play of metaphysics. (GA46, 1938–39: 204–5).

If presence in the broad sense includes becoming, it must also include potential. As Aristotle argues, excluding potency from being means denying the capacity for change and affirming Eleatic immobility (*Met.* IX.3). Potency is present in a changeable being even when it is not changing (GA33, 1931: 219). In change, potency emerges as present without yet being consummated in the achievement of a goal (*Physics* III.1): During the construction of a table, "wood is now *present* in its readiness to become a table" (GA22, 1926: 320).

Unlike Eleatic simplicity, the broad sense of presence also includes multiplicity and relation:

> In the sense of presence there lies the further determination that, if a being is manifold, then there is always a being *and* [another] being, insofar as it has *copresentness* ... Strictly speaking, nothing unique and individual can "be" as a being on its own, for as a unique individual it already lives, as it were, by excluding everything absent, and thus in connection with it. (GA36/37, 1933–34: 115)

As for readiness-to-hand, we might expect it to transcend presence, since we understand a corkscrew in terms of what we can do with it, not simply in terms of what it now is. But Heidegger consistently includes readiness-to-hand in presence. "The understanding of relevance that the use of equipment makes possible is a retained awaiting [*gewärtigen*] in which this particular equipment is made present [*gegenwärtigt*]. In the making-present that expects and retains, the equipment is encountered, becomes present, comes into a present or an awaiting-toward [*Gegen-wart*]" (GA24, 1927: 416). "Readiness-to-hand [is] a Presence of a particular kind" (GA24: 439). It is "a founded Presence ... grounded in the Presence of what is set into care" (GA20, 1925: 264). Nearly four decades later, Heidegger reiterates that "readiness-to-hand as well as at-handness are modes of presence" (GA14, 1962: 11/7). So we cannot escape presence simply by recognizing the importance of coping with useful things – and it is not the case that "presence" in Heidegger requires "thought-mediated intellectual detachment from the world around us" (Noë, 2012: 8).

Heidegger offers more descriptions of broad presence in his accounts of "pre-sentification." "Making-present" (*gegenwärtigen*) is an encounter with something directly, sensibly given. The broader "presentifying" (*vergegenwärtigen*) means bringing something that is not bodily present into the sphere of our awareness (GA20, 1925: 54, 59; GA34, 1932: 296, 307). In Helsinki, I can think of Dubai. (The German expression is not as recondite as the English. It can also be translated as "picturing," "imagining," "recollecting," or "representing," depending on the context.)

Heidegger always insists that presentifying is not about inner representations. When I imagine Dubai, I am bringing the city itself into my purview, not considering or referring to a mark in my brain or mind. My intentionality concerns an entity other than myself (GA20, 1925: 45, 54; GA24, 1927: 98; GA26, 1928: 157; GA34, 1932: 297; GA48, 1940: 193; GA89, 1965: 263–64/68–69).

Presentification is sometimes remembering, and of course requires earlier experience, but it does not necessarily refer to the past (GA83, 1930–31: 277; GA34, 1932: 297; GA83, 1950–51: 479). Its essential function is to draw the absent into the domain of presence (GA35, 1932: 176). It operates, as it were, in a "tele-clearing" (Braver, 2014: 58).

Heidegger also distinguishes presentifying a bygone (*vergangen*) event from recollecting (*andenken*) what has been (*das Gewesene*) (GA46, 1938–39: 40–41). The proper relation to the authentic past does not turn "what is no more" into something present, even in an extended sense, but recollects it in its ongoing significance and relevance – which is futural rather than present (GA51, 1941: 86; GA4, 1943: 100/123).

> Merely presentifying the bygone ... enslaves us to the transitory, tears us away into the evanescent, and perverts us, reducing us to grubbing about and calculating with whatever is left. But recollective intimacy [*Er-innerung*] brings what has been back to us, first shows us the bygone in its essence, and through it, raises us beyond ourselves into the clarity of our destiny. (GA16, 1939: 353–54)

This thought often recurs (GA49, 1941: 10; GA71, 1942: 302; GA4, 1943: 96/119; GA9, 1946: 335/255; GA8, 1952: 161; GA16, 1952: 481). It implies a critique of historiography (*Historie*) as "the presentification of the historical" (*des Geschichtlichen*). Such a project "may still be inevitable for us," but it is not an adequate relation to history proper (GA5, 1946: 327; cf. GA46, 1938–39, 153; GA73.1: 791).

Let's step back now. Has our journey through narrower and broader accounts of presence established what, in general, presence means? To say that being is presence is to claim that presence is the difference it makes to us that there is something instead of nothing. But what is that difference? We have seen that some of Heidegger's characterizations are very narrow, even Eleatic. But in other passages, presence includes change, absence, and other non-Eleatic phenomena. Is there a single concept of presence that runs through both narrow and broad accounts?

The question is extraordinarily hard to answer without appealing to presence itself as a primal concept, or invoking terms that are compromised by their roles in metaphysics: "existence," "actuality," "reality." There is also the risk that seeking a single meaning may itself be a way of insisting on presence (Sallis, 1984: 601). Nevertheless, it is fair to say that presence always involves *display* or *deployment*: What is present is not folded up in undeveloped obscurity, but unfolded so it lies accessibly in the open.

This is not to be understood subjectively, to mean that things have appeared to a mind: "What is present does not first become such when the human notices it" (GA78, 1942: 59). Rather, a present being is "there" rather than nowhere. It shines forth, instead of being swallowed up in nothingness. This is why we can notice it – not vice versa (GA49, 1941: 46). I can see or picture Dubai only because it is already present.

To be clear: The meaning of being as presence needs us, as does all *being* in Heidegger's sense. But when, thanks to this meaning of being, we understand *beings* as present, we experience them as *not* needing us. Being as presence requires Dasein; what is present does not.

Heidegger sometimes unites broader and narrower senses of presence by tracing the degeneration of *presencing* into static *presentness*. This is a tendency, not a necessity; we can recover the original experience of presencing and resist the slide into presentness.

The degeneration can be described both phenomenologically and historically. Phenomenologically, the experience of peak presencing – when something is most fully there – seems to rise above the previous and subsequent moments of incomplete presencing. The apex presentation of an entity shines as its truest manifestation, like the noonday sun. Other moments may then fall into neglect; only full presentness makes a difference. The phenomenon of shining, lasting, and lingering generates an ideal of perfect permanence. "*Presentness* is the *present* in the sense of the collectedness of endurance, in accordance with its drawing back from the transports [of past and future], which are thus displaced and forgotten. This is how the semblance of the *time-lessness* of what genuinely 'is' arises" (GA65, 1936–38: 192).

Historically, we can speculate that although the early Greeks appreciated the whole range of presencing, they fell prey to the tendency we have described, and fixated on full presentness and permanence as the gold standard for being. But not all cultures have adopted this sense of being, so there must be a specifically Greek experience of being as permanence, which is documented in Parmenides. If such an experience is the gift of a mysterious event, as Heidegger tends to believe, it cannot fully be understood. In particular, it cannot be explained simply as a bulwark against impermanence. "Why does what arises and passes away count as what is not? Only if beingness already stands firm as permanence and presentness" (GA65, 1936–38: 195; cf. GA18, 1924: 289). To experience becoming as a *problem* already betrays a conception of being as changeless.

But before we delve further into Heidegger's "history of being," we should look more closely into why he initially resists being as presence, and whether he continues to resist.

4 Heidegger's Developing Thought on Presence

My dog and I are hiking through the woods. Birds call from the high trees that shade our trail. A stream runs below. She barks at me until I pick up a stick. Then she twirls in excitement and lunges at it. I keep snatching the stick away until I finally throw it. She races after it in delight, and I delight in her delight.

Be here now, *I tell myself.*

But what allows my dog and me to be here now is our not-nows. Our habits let us follow the trail and recognize birdsongs. Our anticipation incites us to discover more. We inhabit this moment thanks to past and possibility.

And for me, it's harder to be immersed in the hike than it is for her. I catch myself daydreaming, reviewing personal and professional challenges, worrying about politics. I can't manage simply to taste the moment; when I try, I savor my very tasting, I enjoy the dog's enjoyment, and I reflect until the pleasure is dulled. I even imagine drawing on this experience to make a philosophical point. Then I remind myself: Be here now.

Be: but what does that mean? The dog is, and has no need to tell herself to be. Being must mean a great deal to her, but she lives in that meaning without the desire or ability to articulate it, while I am blessed or cursed with distance. I cannot be without calling being into question.

I fail to be fully present. Or should I say I can't be reduced *to full presence? Am I too expansive to fit within the confines of the here and now? Or is it better to*

say that the here and now is a limited presence, while full presence means inhabiting a larger temporal scope?
She barks at me again. I snap out of my ruminations and continue on the path.

If we take presence in the broad sense as "presencing," is there still an edge to Heidegger's statement "being is presence"? Did his early critique give way to acceptance? So far, I have offered most evidence with minimal context, simply to establish the range of meanings that "presence" can have. The question now is how Heidegger works with those meanings to develop a critical perspective that may or may not eventually be blunted. We can divide his thought into three phases as we look for continuities and transformation.

4.1 Heidegger's Early Critique: Presence and Time

Heidegger's "thunderbolt" (GA82, 1943: 355) gave him "the decisive hint that being, in some concealed way, stands in the clearing of time" (GA16, 1946: 424). His work of the 1920s develops the idea that presence is available to us through the present, as a dimension of Dasein's existential temporality. This implies a critique of the Western tradition, which has privileged presence and interpreted time in terms of it, distorting or neglecting other ways of being – especially the being of Dasein itself. This critique provides the energy and the guiding thread for reading his predecessors. "In the same moment as I recognized that *einai–ousia* names presence in the unconcealed, and itself essences as presentness (*parousia*) on the basis of 'time,' the early destiny of being was already experienced: the oblivion of the truth of being as the being of truth" (GA82, ca. late 1940s: 217).

But these are retrospective judgments. When did the thunderbolt strike? We cannot say exactly, but as early as 1913, storm clouds are gathering. Young Heidegger writes: "I must have something in the present [*gegenwärtig*] in order to reject it, i.e. posit it as not in being. The indefiniteness of the words 'acknowledge' and 'reject' also involves an indefiniteness of the concept 'existence'" (GA1: 123).

The connection between presence and time coalesces in the early twenties. Heidegger reflects on the Platonic concept of "the presentness (*parousia*) of the supratemporal in temporal beings" (GA60, 1920–21: 45) and investigates "how we originally experience temporality in factical experience" (GA60: 65). "Factical life" must be understood in terms of its time (GA61, 1921–22: 176), which is "*kairological*" (GA63, 1923: 101) – punctuated by significant moments.

By 1923, the lightning has struck – and with the help of a parallel between Greek and German, Heidegger finds a clue to the origin of being as presence in everyday dealings. In Greek thought, "*ousia* provides the basic character of what *is* as . . . *presentness*. It is implicitly included in the [everyday] concepts of 'things'" (GA17, 1923: 46). *Ousia* is formed from *ous-* (the root of the feminine present participle of *einai*, to be) and the feminine abstract ending *-ia*. It literally means "beingness"; the German grammatical equivalent would be the contrived formation *Seiendheit* (GA31, 1930: 47, 50). But in everyday Greek, *ousia* is not a high-flying theoretical term; it refers to property (compare the expression "real estate"). *Ousia* is "what one manages in everyday Dasein, what stands there available. Being means: standing available" (GA19, 1924–25: 270). "This seemingly so abstract philosophical concept means belongings, assets, what is around me at home, '*Anwesen*'" (GA17: 46). Like *ousia*, *Anwesen* normally means property or estate – but especially with the addition of the abstract ending *-heit*, it also refers to presence (for instance, the attendance of people at an event).

On their own, these linguistic facts would be a tenuous basis for analyzing the entire Western understanding of being, but a little phenomenology makes Heidegger's point more plausible. As I get ready to cook, I open the cupboard and reach for my frying pan. It's right where I left it, right where I keep it. I feel its familiar heft as I place it on the stove. The pan is present: It's available as part of my handy supply of things I own and use. Its handiness concerns both *what* it is and *that* it is: Its very essence is to be useful, and if it were missing from my cupboard, it would be unavailable. It is accessible not just for frying, but for observation: I can, on occasion, just look at the pan as there at hand.

Based on such ordinary interactions with possessions, we can develop an inarticulate sense that everything that *is*, is at hand or ready-to-hand – in a word, present. We do not perceive everything as an artifact, but we experience even what is not manmade with reference to utility. In his breakthrough text "The Concept of Time" (1924), Heidegger develops a meticulous vocabulary for these experiences.

> The "aroundness" that is always already at hand, e.g. as house and home, *intrinsically* includes the whereupon and where of "property/presence" ["*Anwesen*"]: soil, field, forest, mountain, river, and everything under the sky. The environment of these things that are at hand every day ... is encountered with the same character as the world of concern. It is there as that *on which* concern counts (the presentness, course, and setting of the sun, phases of the moon, weather), what it protects itself from (in housebuilding), what it uses, what provides material for production (wood, bronze), or as a way and means of business and travel (water, wind) ... Even the

presentness of "nature" comes to appearance in its most real at-handness with the characteristic referential contexts that concern has disclosed ... What we immediately encounter comes to the fore from the aroundness of the world that is already present in advance, reliably, undetached in its Presence. (GA64, 1924: 22–23)

Heidegger's painstaking phenomenology culminates in *Being and Time*'s celebrated account of the "environment." Other interpreters, especially Hubert Dreyfus (1991), have discussed that account far more fully than I can here. For our purposes, what matters is that the interpretation of being as presence is "natural and naive, because this sense of being ... is taken as the absolute sense of being simply" (GA19, 1924–25: 270). To take presence as our paradigm is to distort the being of other kinds of entities – ourselves in particular. In our practical concerns, we attach ourselves to the present, forgetting "what has been" and "being-futural" (GA64: 65). "What is present is encountered in the present: it is encountered by the disclosure and interpretation of the world that says 'now'"; the now-saying Dasein "interprets itself" – that is, *mis*interprets itself – "on the basis of the world as what is accessibly present" (GA64: 74). I am the owner of my house, the cook, or the breadwinner – and I am present here, like my house and my frying pan. In this everyday sense of being, I am oblivious to my own temporality.

> [The] primary at-handness must be understood as *presentness, Presence*. Why? [The] relationship to beings as beings is a relationship that ... has a present-oriented [*präsentisch*] character ... A relationship is present-oriented if it has the sense of presenting [*präsentieren*], or as we say in German, *making-present* [*gegenwärtigen*] ... This making-present, *in which I constantly live* ... gives me the possibility of encountering anything at all, i.e. the possibility that something that presences is discoverable, can be present ... The present is *a characteristic of time* ... The Greeks suspected nothing of this abyssal problematic. (GA21, 1925–26: 191–93)

This passage bases being-at-hand on the making-present that is part of daily life and that is apparent in our "concern with what is producible and available" (GA21: 412).

For Dreyfus, Heidegger grounds being-at-hand in "'mindless' everyday coping skills as the basis of all intelligibility" (1991: 3). But both practical coping and theoretical staring are "present-oriented"; they disregard the greater reach of time. Both attitudes are subordinate to temporal "care" (SZ: 193, 364). If there is any way for time and care themselves to become intelligible, then no present-oriented behavior can be the ground of *all* intelligibility. Heidegger's account of this behavior is not a foundation, but the start of an excavation – or rather, a first step into the "abyssal problematic" of time, which may have no certain ground at all. "It never occurred to me ... to try to prove ... that the essence of the human consists in the fact that we handle spoons and forks and ride the streetcar" (GA29/30, 1929–30: 263). To the contrary, traditional ontology is *inappropriately* based on utility and production (GA24, 1927: 147–48, 153).

This is not inconsistent with the idea that traditional ontology is based on contemplation, if contemplation is an offshoot of production and both occur within the sphere of presence. Heidegger offers several, perhaps compatible accounts of just how this works. The long passage I quoted from GA64: 22–23 describes how nature comes forth as at-hand because our familiar environment depends on it. Heidegger also sometimes proposes that a product, once produced, becomes "available in itself" and "constantly present on its own" (GA24, 1927: 210); it can then be observed as at-hand. (Later texts refer to this as the *Herstand* or "standing-forth" of a produced thing, which then becomes a *Gegenstand* or "object" [GA79, 1949: 7; GA80.2, 1950: 956].) Another proposal is that contemplating what is at hand begins with a "deficiency" in using the ready-to-hand (SZ: 61). In the present, we make and handle useful things; those things can go missing, or become inconvenient or unusable; they may then appear as merely at hand, as finished and static objects that call for inspection; and this becomes the standard concept of being in the tradition.

Both contemplation and use operate within the horizonal schema of Presence (GA24: 433, 436), but Presence presupposes time. So rather than establishing use as the fundamental way to make sense of things, Heidegger looks to a broader temporal horizon that makes Presence possible. From this perspective, the difference between at-handness and readiness-to-hand is less crucial than it initially seems.

Time is triply ecstatic, but we tend to fall into one ecstasis – the present. Naturally enough, we get fascinated by what we are doing now and what stands before us. "Essentially falling, temporality loses itself in making-present [and understands itself] in terms of the ready-to-hand entities with which it is concerned" (SZ: 369). The risk is that we will then understand everything merely as something to be manipulated or observed, and misunderstand ourselves as mere manipulators and observers. Our own being is always at issue, but we work out this issue by engaging with other beings; how easy it is, then, to identify ourselves with what we do, handle, or observe. We view ourselves as just another thing of concern, present in an immediately accessible now. "We are usually lost in the present, and it seems as if the future and the past – or more precisely, having-been – have dimmed down, as if Dasein were leaping into the present at each moment. This is an illusion" (GA24, 1927: 376) – because without future and past, the present would be impossible.

Heidegger's description of authentic temporality strains to find language that is not bound to the present: "Futurally coming back to itself, resoluteness brings itself into the Situation as it makes present. Having-been arises from the future, in such a way that the future that has been (or rather, is been-ing [*gewesende*]), releases the present from itself" (SZ: 326). He writes here at the limits of grammar (cf. SZ: 39) because the tense system is ill-suited to describing the interplay of the dimensions of time.

Immersed in the present, we interpret time itself in terms of presence. We track changes by way of things now at hand (a shadow on a sundial, the hands of a clock); this seduces us into taking time itself, or at least the now, as a present entity (SZ: 417). We take the future as not yet present, the past as no longer present (GA64, 1924: 101). This perspective gets things backward by subordinating time to presence – and inevitably misconstrues our *own* way of being as temporal entities.

Heidegger's critique is not aimed simply at an atemporal eternity. Recall that he describes a broad sense of presence – including readiness-to-hand, absence, change, and the "presentifying" of remote things – in several texts of the 1920s. No matter how diverse these phenomena may be, if they are encountered within a present-oriented horizon, they cannot address time as Heidegger understands it. In particular, an experience of flux that remains within the sphere of presence is inadequate.

This is not to say we should abandon presence. Instead, we should seize it more fully, in the context of past and future. This is the resolute, disclosed temporality that Heidegger calls "the moment." "The moment is a making-present of something present that belongs to the resolution and discloses the situation into which resoluteness has resolved itself" (GA24, 1927: 407). A crisis removes me from my routine micro-concerns, challenging me to grapple with who I am to be; in a resolute moment, I grasp my whole life and take action.

Derrida's early reading of *Being and Time* (1964) sums up Heidegger's critique: "the present [is] the past of a future" (Derrida, 2016: 188). There can be no simple, self-evident "is," but rather a "will have been," or many "will have beens." (Derrida's predilection for the future perfect seems like an affectation until one understands its Heideggerian grounds.) "What will be grasped under the name historical past is something that will never have been first *present* ... [The historian] must repeat toward a past that was also an opening toward the future, which never was a present and positive fact" (Derrida, 2016: 213). Deconstruction traces how any attempt to establish presence undermines itself, betraying its indebtedness to the history it would like to bury and the opening it would like to deny. Deconstruction reminds the present that presence is not self-certifying.

Derridean thinking is centrifugal: It draws us away from any reliance on a supposedly full presence, into proliferating series of differences and deferrals. In contrast, Heidegger thinks centripetally: Authentic temporality can gather us, even if briefly, into a resolute moment. Is this a remnant of the priority of presence?

4.2 Heidegger's Middle Critique: Presence and Appropriation

When we turn to Heidegger's middle period, roughly from 1930 to the early 1940s, we find a good deal of continuity with his earlier critique of presence. In 1934, he says, "The now was taken as the core of time ... But now that we have established how time temporalizes from the future and from having-been, we have leapt over the present as the evanescent. Here a complete transformation of the essence of being comes to light" (GA38: 123). In 1938–39, he writes, "The only 'being' that metaphysics knows, the constancy of presencing, is only a still ungrounded selection of *one* essential moment of being, in-the-presentness [*Gegenwärtigkeit*], which is never recognized in its essencing as 'temporality'" (GA66: 394). Or consider these notes from 1941:

> For Western thinking, what is present, what is in the present, has long counted and still counts today as that which is. But what is yet to come already *is* in its coming. Even what has been still *is* ...What is in the present first arises from the encounter between future and provenance. This is what apparently leaps out of the encounter and spreads open on its own, creating the illusion that only what is now present is a being. (GA50: 147).

Heidegger's targets here surely include conceptions that acknowledge the being of past and future, but misinterpret them as forms of presence.

Heidegger challenges us to broaden our conception of being so that it embraces what it has come to exclude. For us, "What is at hand and is present counts as what is. So wherever we encounter what is apparently 'negative,' we find it hard not to just look at the 'positive,' instead of grasping something more original above and beyond this distinction" (GA45, 1937–38: 152). A more original sense of being would include what we ordinarily see as nonpresent or deficiently present. Thus, *Introduction to Metaphysics* traces the opposition of being to becoming, seeming, thinking, and the "ought," and describes the meaning of "being" in these oppositions as "*constant presentness*" (GA40, 1935: 211/225). But if becoming, seeming, thinking, and the "ought" are something and not nothing, they must *be* in some sense other than constant presence. "*So the concept of being that has been accepted up to now does not suffice to name everything that 'is'*" (GA40: 213/227).

Many statements from the thirties and forties confirm that Heidegger's stance toward presence is still critical – sometimes combative, sometimes elegiac. "The question [is] why the [Greek] inception must grasp being qua presentness, why the inception gets intercepted!" (GA35, 1932: 73). "What must be questioned is the full essence of being – presentness (the 'is') positively fused into it, and at the same time the predominance [of presentness] beaten back into its limits" (GA94, ca. 1932: 51). "The mood of the [new] inception [is] *the concealed deep mourning over the veiled decay of essence into being as presentness*" (GA94, ca. 1932: 72). "'Beyng' means ... beyng in its original essencing ... not limited to 'presentness'" (GA65, 1936–38: 75). "The first inception thinks beyng as presentness on the basis of presencing, which constitutes the first flaring up of *one* essencing of beyng" (GA65: 31). "Essencing, not grasped as such, is presencing" (GA65: 189). "A long faded gleam of essencing is presence" (GA97, 1940s: 218).

This is all consistent with Heidegger's work of the twenties, but he is now less confident about the character of time. "What is time itself, so that it can shine as this light that illuminates being? How do being and time come into this original connection? What is this connection? What does time mean? What does being mean? What, above all, does being *and* time mean?" (GA31, 1931: 115). "'Presentness' and 'permanence' are evidently temporal determinations [but] it becomes ever more obscure in what sense here 'temporal determination' and 'time' are to be thought" (GA82, 1941: 296).

The reasons for the collapse of *Being and Time* I.3, which was to spell out the meaning of being in terms of time, are complex and debatable (Braver, 2015). But one suggestive slogan describes a shift "from the understanding of being to the *happening of being*" (GA40, 1935: 218). Time is no longer a "transcendental horizon" (SZ: 39) that determines the meaning of being: Heidegger drops the quasi-Kantian idea that Dasein's temporality delineates "schemata" in terms of which various kinds of being can be understood (SZ: 365; GA24, 1927: 436). This approach seems static, ahistorical, and subjectivist; it is replaced by the "happening of being" as a movement that engages and carries us.

This happening is "momentaneous"; if it could be viewed from the outside, it would appear as "only a fleeting minute of 'world history' – in the immense infinity of times and spaces, it flashes and is then extinguished" (GA73.1, ca. 1930s: 207). But at this moment, being in general and our own being become an issue (GA40, 1935: 6–7/5–6). This happening is "the ground of our self" (GA73.1: 445). What is at stake is "the grounding of Da-sein as the site of the happening of being" (GA82, 1936: 31).

The "happening of being" can also be called *das Ereignis*, "the event of appropriation" (GA73.1: 258; GA82, 1936: 197). *Ereignis* is how beyng essences (GA65, 1936–38: 183, 344); it is short for *das Ereignis der Dagründung*, the event of the grounding of the there (GA65: 183, 247). This eruption of "time-space" enables us to inhabit a where and a when (GA65: 379–88; Polt, 2006: 180–92). It gives us an understanding of beings in their beingness.

But what is the status of Heidegger's descriptions of this "happening"? Is he observing it like any other phenomenon? That would threaten to bring *Ereignis* within the ambit of presence, whereas (like temporality in the earlier work) it is supposed to be the condition of possibility for presence – not in a transcendental sense, but as a concealed event (e.g., GA65: 174).

This problem is one motive for a new conception of philosophy in the 1930s: Philosophy is not just the observation of a present given, but helps beyng take place. "Philosophy brings about the inner intensification of the happening of being, and thus of Dasein in its breadth and depth" (GA94, ca. 1931: 29). Philosophy's task is "the awakening of the happening of being" (GA94: 59). "Inceptive thinking is the inventive thinking [*Er-denken*] of the truth of beyng, and thus the bringing about of the ground [*Ergründung des Grundes*]" (GA65, 1936–38: 56). It "brings beyng into the truth of its essencing" (GA65: 108). Such thinking does not arbitrarily invent beyng, but "exposes itself questioningly to beyng" (GA65: 86). They happen together. At an extreme, we could say that thinking *is* the event of appropriation, and vice versa: "the saying here is not opposed to what is to be said, but is this itself as the essencing of beyng" (GA65: 4; cf. GA66, 1938–39: 51, 64).

Since Dasein requires the happening of beyng, inventively thinking this happening means venturing Dasein as a *possibility*, not a fact. Dasein is "the ground of a particular, coming way to be human, not of 'humanity' in itself" (GA65: 300). This point is stated most starkly and uncompromisingly in Heidegger's 1936 running notes on *Being and Time* (Polt, 2020): "In *Being and Time*, Dasein and being-human [are] equated ... instead, Dasein ... 'is' only in this happening of the leap" (GA82: 22).

A text dated 1937 summarizes the critique of presence in Heidegger's middle thought.

> Why *this* interpretation [of being as presentness]? Because here it is most graspable, conceivable, and handy – to begin with, in what is at hand, what lies before the hand ... But presentness stems from presencing, which arises from the futurizing-beening, captivating-transporting in the time-space of the strife between world and earth as the clearing concealing of the there – insofar as Da-*sein* becomes steadfast [*inständig*] on the ground of appropriation by the (event). (GA73.1: 96)

This last sentence packs together many challenging concepts to suggest the rich happening that lets us have the seemingly straightforward experience of encountering something before us. Say a glass of water stands on a table before me, present now as a relatively stable thing. Its presentness is not self-sufficient: It arises within a larger sphere of presence, a context – it's mid-afternoon on a summer day, and I have the water within reach on my desk as I work. I am capably absorbed in my workspace, while I rely on habits and possibilities to let me understand what I am doing. I inhabit a world – a complex of meanings and purposes that I share with others – in which a glass of water is a recognized object with accepted uses. This world rests on the earth: Though I often ignore it, the earth provides water, shelter, materials for glassmaking, and so on – but it also exceeds the uses we make of it and the knowledge we gain about it. My "there" has opened up for me as a place where I belong and encounter beings, though never in full, and never without error and oblivion. Or *do* I belong? *Do* I genuinely encounter things? Perhaps not unless I become "steadfast" by heeding these contexts for presence and engaging in them appropriately, instead of simply looking at, and looking after, the things before me.

What sort of engagement is "steadfast"? In Heidegger's most political phase, it takes the form of labor:

> In labor as the present [*Gegenwart*] in the sense of making-present [*Gegenwärtigung*], the present-making [*Anwesendmachen*] of beings happens. Labor is the present in the original sense that we presently await [*entgegenwarten*] what is, and thus let it come over us in its historicity; we comply with its superior power, we govern it in the great mood of struggle, admiration, and honor, and enhance it in its greatness. (GA38, 1934: 154)

Authentic work, like *Being and Time*'s "moment," integrates the present into a broader temporal sweep. We might think here of building a structure where major cultural or political events might take place, or of artwork more generally. Genuine engagement is a polemical, turbulent process that we may be tempted to resist by fixating on permanence and presence, which are "the closest and sole ground that resists the abyss" (GA66, 1938–39: 92).

What is present can be inspected and reinspected by sight. In his middle period, Heidegger develops his critique of the traditional priority of seeing. The ancient Greeks are famous for their keen visual sense. Homer gives us a vivid "procession of phenomena [that] takes place in the foreground – that is, in a local and temporal present that is absolute" (Auerbach, 1953: 7). It is no accident that *theoria* means viewing; that "I know," *oida*, means "I have seen"; and that *idea* and *eidos*, words for the "look" of things, come to mean their essence, how they appear to the mind's eye. Heidegger's link between the preeminence of vision and the rule of presence has influenced later continental philosophy, particularly in France (Jay, 1993). "Due to its extraordinary character of *making-Present* [*Präsent-machen*], sensory seeing comes to play the role of the definitive example of knowing, taken as the grasping of what is. The essence of seeing is that it makes things be in the present and holds them there" (GA34, 1931–32: 159–60). On the one hand, the prior Greek sense of being as presence and constancy gives seeing this role (GA48, 1940: 299–300; GA88, 1941–42: 190). On the other hand, a certain human way of looking "first makes presence possible and is more original than the presentness of things" (GA54, 1942–43: 158).

"The optical essences within the ecstatic" (GA97, 1940s: 423). So to do justice to ecstatic time, we must break free of vision as the model for thinking. "Just as 'seeing' – *theoria* – was determined by presencing, now beyng as appropriation requires *the word and hearing* [as] the awaiting finding of the coming – i.e. of history" (GA69, 1938–40: 222).

We might recall how Judaism emphasizes hearing the word over seeing the look (Auerbach, 1953: 8–12). We might also think of the problem of "presentism" in historiography (Hartog, 2015; Tamm and Olivier, 2019). But Heidegger disregards the "Hebraic heritage" in his thought (Zarader, 2006) and insists that his *Geschichte* is deeper than any *Historie*: Both historicism and presentism (*Aktualismus*) miss what essentially has-been (GA49, 1941: 10). In his language, the proper or own can be found only through the retrieval of the possible, not the presence of the present or the representation of the bygone.

4.3 Heidegger's Late Thinking: Presence and Letting-Presence

Now we turn to a few features of Heidegger's late thought (beginning around the mid-forties), which according to some readers embraces a form of presence (Blattner, 1999: 289–90; Malpas, 2008: 13; Hernández, 2011).

The retrospective text "Der Weg," from 1943, reviews Heidegger's path. He recalls the "thunderbolt" of glimpsing the connection between being and time (GA82: 355). This "fundamental experience" harbors the possibility of "a transformation of the essence of truth, being, humanity, and all that is" (GA82: 358). The connection between being and time is not exhausted by the book *Being and Time*, whose approach is all too reminiscent of Kant: The problem of time as the condition of possibility for the understanding of being is "a transcendental question squared" (GA82: 350–52). For all the differences between Dasein and the Kantian subject, a residual subjectivism hovers over this project, as if Dasein had a fixed essence that provided the parameters for the meaning of being. Against such subjectivism, "being itself" calls on us to think it, giving us hints (GA82: 354, 357). Those hints include the fact that "from early on," being has meant "the encountering presence-to" (*das angegnende Anwesen*) (GA82: 363).

As for time, it is the "forecourt" (*Vorhof*) (GA82: 348) or "preliminary name" (*Vorname*) (GA82: 353) for what Heidegger now prefers to call "the truth of being" (GA82: 348; cf. GA9, 1949: 376–77/285–86; GA74: 9/6). "Truth" here, of course, does not mean propositional correctness, but unconcealment or clearing. *Being and Time* should perhaps be renamed "clearing and presentness" (GA14, 1964: 90/73). But the clearing involves concealment. Thus "presence (being) belongs in the clearing of self-concealing (time)" (GA11, 1962: 151/ WJR: xx). Since the clearing is characterized by or originates in *Ereignis*, another new name for *Being and Time* might be "presence and appropriation" (GA100, 1950s: 173; cf. 175, 177).

The 1962 lecture "Time and Being" is Heidegger's most public statement on being, time, and appropriation. Here he describes *Ereignis* as the "it" that "gives" both time and being (GA14: 24/19). Time and being as presence mutually determine each other, but appropriation is the source of both. "In the sending of the destiny of being, in the reaching of time, is shown an appropriating, an owning-over of being as presence and time as the realm of the open into what is proper to them. What determines both time and being in what is proper to them, i.e. in their belonging together, we call *appropriation*" (GA14: 24/19).

Of course, "clearing" and "appropriation" are no less in need of interpretation than "time," and whatever time may be, it still plays a central role in Heidegger's thought and his history of metaphysics (Hughes and Stendera, 2024). He does not renounce his early account of Dasein's temporality; he repeats it in the *Zollikon Seminars* of the 1960s (GA89: 179–377/29–67). But he also attempts to rethink it: "Time transports us into ... the unity of having-been, presence, [and] the future"; this threefold unity is time-space (GA12, 1957–58: 201–2/106). Time-space allows meaningful proximity – and thus, presence. So "time is four-dimensional: The *first* dimension, which gathers all, is *nearness*" (GA9, 1949: 377n/286n).

The concept of nearness links time to appropriation and clearing. A clearing is not primarily an illuminated spot, but an opening that has been cleared – a place of clearance. Clearance is room to maneuver – to handle, encounter, and consider things. Since it provides contact with beings, the clearing grants nearness; but it must also involve distance, for a confluence of everything, the ultimate closeness, would be closed rather than open, leaving no space for perspectives and possibilities. Furthermore, for nearness to be significant, it must involve owning or belonging, as well as their opposites. I perceive a piece of trash, over there in the corner of my yard, as alien: It does not belong. I pick it up and discard it. In this everyday experience, there is both appropriation and expropriation, nearness and distance. Time is part of the clearing that allows the trash to be present to me.

In notes from 1947, Heidegger sketches a derivation of Dasein's temporality from the event of beyng itself. The clearing arrives like a "lightning bolt," creating futurity (GA82: 250) – presumably because it opens possibilities. This event involves a differentiation or "bearing apart" (*Austrag*) of being and beings, so that entities appear in a space of meaning; in turn, we are charged with bearing or withstanding this openness. This is the origin of Dasein's "ecstasis" (GA82: 256). But beyng also withdraws: the event of opening fades away, yielding to the presence of present beings. This is the "epochal" character of beyng, which we will consider in Section 5. It, too, must be withstood ecstatically (GA82: 252).

In sum, Heidegger's late thoughts on time set his earlier temporal analysis of being as presence in the context of clearing and appropriation, but he does not abandon this analysis. "The present that holds sway in presence is a characteristic of time" (GA7, 1952: 142).

But what becomes of the earlier critique of presence? "Does being exclusively ... amount to presence, so that its other characteristics can be ignored? The priority of presence ... is a *question* and a task for thinking, namely, to consider whether and whence and to what extent the priority of presence subsists" (GA14, 1962: 42/34).

Some texts sound confident that this question has been settled: As Juan Pablo Hernández puts it, "being is identical with the act of *presencing*" (2011: 234). "Being itself – this means: the presence of what is present" (GA12, 1953–54: 116/30). Even the various ways of being described in *Being and Time* are all modes of presence (GA82, ca. 1967: 401). "But where do we get the right to characterize being as presence? The question comes too late. For this formation of being has long been decided without our contribution, let alone our merit. Since then, we are bound to the characterization of being as presence" (GA14, 1962: 10/6). "Have we invented being (as presence)? Or has it long been found for us, although the find has not been appropriated in the way that befits it?" (GA73.2: 1319).

But other late texts affirm that a different sense of being is possible: "in no way [does being] necessarily appear only as the presentness of what presences" (GA5, 1950: 155/116). "Being itself does not exhaust its essence in essencing as the presence of the present" (GA80.2, 1950: 973). "We would fall prey to an error if we wanted to believe that the being of what *is* means only, and for all times, the presence of what is present" (GA8, 1952: 239/235). In particular, "ek-sistence can never be determined by 'being' qua presence" (GA100, 1952–57: 174). "Presence can always keep creating the illusion that everything to be thought is authentically thought on its basis and in its domain" (GA102, 1963: 43).

How firmly, then, are we tied to presence? Heidegger thinks of the tie between presence and humanity as requirement (*Brauch*). "'Time' [was] the unthought preliminary name for requirement" (GA82: 239). "Only man, open to being, lets it come to him as presence. This presence-to requires [*braucht*] the open of a clearing, and through this requiring it thus remains owned over to the human essence"; *braucht* means both "needs and demands" (GA11, 1957: 40/ ID 31; cf. GA79, 1957: 121).

We can infer that being as presence is not a necessity for all humans at all times, but only for those who are "required" to stand in the legacy of Greek thinking. "This appearing of being as the presence of what is present is itself *the* inception of Western history" (GA7, 1952: 142). Being as presence is a historical necessity – the Western destiny – which, through globalization, is becoming the destiny of the planet.

Of course, escaping destiny is no simple matter, and seeking a different sense of being may not be the right approach. "The *awkward and misleading* talk of how presence does not constitute the only way of 'being.' (Necessary for a first understanding! But is that needed?) *In this way*, 'being' is held fast, raised to an even higher level, instead of twisting free (and crossing out) – and even *that* is insufficient" (GA98, ca. 1950: 326). "Twisting free" translates *Verwindung* – not *Überwindung*, overcoming or triumph, but a winding-out in which one convalesces or deals with a difficult experience (GA70, 1941: 19–20/11).

If we twist free from being, where do we turn? "Twisting free of being (presence) as such into expropriation [*Enteignis*]. Vanishing of being; completion of the destiny of being; its end" (GA73.2: 1356).

> Presence ("being"), as presence, is always presence to the human essence, insofar as presence is a summons that in each case calls to the human essence. The human essence as such listens, because it hears and belongs to the calling summons, the presence-to. This, which is the selfsame every time, the belonging together of call and listening – would that then be "being"? What am I saying? It is in no way "being" anymore – if we try to think through "being" as it holds sway in our destiny, namely, as presence, which is the only way we can correspond to its destinal essence. (GA9, 1955: 408/308–9)

We must primarily consider not being or presence, but the source of our intimacy with presence, our belonging with it. We are to turn our attention from *Anwesen* to *Anwesen-lassen*: letting-presence, allowing presence (e.g., GA14, 1962: 9/5, 46; GA15, 1969: 365/60; GA102, 1963–70: 47, 161–62). What allows presence, as we have seen, can be called the clearing. "The clearing, as the affording of free space for presence, and for the lingering of what is present, is neither something present nor a property of presentness ... That and how the clearing affords presentness: considering this belongs to the question of the determination of the matter for thinking" (GA16, 1965: 630/ QCD 220).

Such statements leave several questions unresolved. Granted that the clearing is not an achievement of subjectivity, doesn't it still function as a transcendental condition of the possibility of experience? How does it differ from the early notion of Presence as the field in which entities can appear as present? Does a solution lie in some reciprocity between the clearing and what appears in it – much as, in the *Contributions to Philosophy*, beyng is "simultaneous" with beings and truth needs to be "sheltered" in them (Polt, 2006: 193–202)?

In seeking the source of presence itself, does Heidegger head away from experience, longing for an inaccessible event, intimating what cannot be given? If so, is this fruitless speculation or a heroic application of the principle of sufficient reason, which refuses to rest satisfied with appearances and keeps asking, even in the face of silence: Why? Near the end, Heidegger asked himself, "Is it enough to distinguish between letting *presence* and *letting presence*? ... Or does this characterization still tend toward the representation of a first ground?" (GA102, 1970: 347).

We can also think of letting-presence via *Ereignis*. In its usual sense, *Ereignis* means an ordinary event as "a kind of presence of what is present" (GA99, late 1940s: 114); but as the *source* of being as presence, it is not present at all, but is a "twisting free of 'being'" (GA100, 1952–57: 59). "'Being,' that is, presentness, is taken back into the appropriating that is already owning in advance within presentness" (GA91: 690). "Only in the suddenness of the appropriating of the difference does the 'is' take place [*ereignet sich*], as does the presence of what is present" (GA99, 1947–50: 53). This is the "genealogy of the essence of presence in terms of appropriation" (GA99: 54). "B̶e̶y̶n̶g̶ [crossed out] [is] twisted free into owness" (GA101, 1957–59: 136).

But now, a twist returns us to the possibility of expanding the meaning of being. If letting-presence is thought as appropriation, then "what is present will itself be transformed into what is appropriated – what is befitted in the befitting [*Befugte der Befugnis*] of the fourfold – what is p̶r̶e̶s̶e̶n̶t̶ [crossed out] in the fourfold is 'the thing' in the lecture on the thing, which looks forward" (GA73.2: 1295).

Heidegger refers here to his 1949 Bremen lectures – his only postwar public discourses that, in 1964, he called nonmetaphysical (Sinn, 1991: 172). In his well-known example, a "thing" such as a jug reflects "the fourfold" (Mitchell, 2015): With the jug, *mortals* offer a libation to *divinities*, pouring *earth*-given wine beneath the bounteous *sky* (GA79: 11–13). This vision is no description of our current experience; it smacks of both nostalgia and utopia. "Things are long gone, and yet they have never been *as things*" (GA79: 23). "Are things still around us? Have things ever yet been as things?" (GA80.2, 1950: 949).

"The Thing" asserts that "all representing of what is present in the sense of what stands forth and stands against us as an object never reaches the thing as thing" (GA79: 7). Conversely, "From the thinging of the thing there takes place [*ereignet sich*] and is first determined even the presence of what is present like a jug" (GA79: 16). If thinging determines presence, and the very word "present" is to be crossed out when we think the thing, then the thing would no longer be under the sway of presence. Yet it still would *be* – in a rich way that indicates the four dimensions of the fourfold (another meaning of the device of crossing out a word; GA9, 1955: 411/311). Presence would not vanish, but would be enfolded in a richer happening, "a multidimensional background that as such remains *nonpresent*" (Backman, 2015: 8).

Why do we not have "things" around us? What prevents them from "thinging" is *Verwahrlosung*: "unprotectedness" or "loss of truth." The 1949 lecture attributes unprotectedness to objectification, or to im-position (*Ge-stell*) as the essence of technological revealing (GA79: 47). But a "more didactic" version of the lecture, written in 1950 but published only seventy years later, reaches a more radical thought.

> The unprotectedness of the thing is as old as the inceptive clearing of being, in accordance with which being takes place as the presence of what is present . . . The unprotectedness of the thing is thus not a consequence of the reign of the ob-jective and the distanceless [the homogeneous, flat objectivity of our age], but vice versa: the reign of the distanceless, and with it the lack of nearness, is an essential consequence of the unprotectedness of the thing that secretly holds sway in the beginning of the clearing of being. (GA80.2: 971)

Presence itself, from the start, crowds out the rich relationality of "things." This passage echoes Heidegger's very early analysis of the origin of presence in ordinary experience: "*ousia* provides the basic character of what *is* as . . . *presentness*. It is implicitly included in the [everyday] concepts of 'things'" (GA17, 1923: 46). Supposedly, then, until the fateful extraction of presence from practice, the Greeks experienced thinging. "What is present appears early on in the thing, but only late [that is, in the future] *as* the thing" (GA98, 1948–51: 397).

Summing up: Heidegger's late thought often lets being equal presence, because that is its historical destiny. He turns to what *allows* presence, which we may call clearing or appropriation. But this thinking may transform what is present into "things" within the fourfold. If "being" is the difference it makes to us that there is something instead of nothing, then this experience of "things" would be a transformation of being – a new (or very ancient) import of what *is*. This meaning of being would be less reductive, more disclosive, richer than presence. It turns out, then, that Heidegger does want to expand the meaning of being beyond presence, after all.

5 Presence in the History of Being

I was at the piano yesterday, experimenting with some favorite chord sequences, when I hit upon a rhythm and melody that enticed me. The sounds repeated until my left hand's shift from one chord to the next became fluid and thoughtless, and the tune my right hand played developed into a hypnotic cycle. It continued until the momentum faded and I let it drift away.

Was I myself in those moments? It doesn't matter. I was submerged in the music. There was no need to be self-conscious, any more than to name the chords or visualize the melody. No words or pictures were required. These words come after the fact – and they can only point to the experience, failing to revive the melody, reminding me of what did not ask to be remembered but simply was.

The word "presence" applies only in retrospect.

The upshot of our wanderings through Heidegger's texts is not a doctrine of presence. Maybe insisting on a doctrine is itself a symptom of the obsession with presence. And even if we could identify such a doctrine, it would be less significant than the underlying questions and motives. Still, there is good reason to doubt that he came to accept presence as the meaning of being. Presence remains problematic because it may crowd out certain kinds of beings, and it distracts us from its source in "time," "appropriation," "requirement," or "the clearing."

We have frequently touched on Heidegger's critique of the Western tradition, and pointed out that his thought on presence is never simply phenomenological but always has a historical dimension. What we have not yet considered closely is what "historical" means, and just what he intends when, beginning in the 1930s, he speaks of "the history of being." As we will see, this does not simply mean a doxography – an account, no matter how critical, of the opinions of past philosophers.

5.1 The Concept of the History of Being

Seinsgeschichte is best approached, initially, through the distinction between *Geschichte* and *Historie* (SZ: 375–76, 392–97). *Geschichte* is Dasein's shared temporality: Each generation draws on its heritage as it works out its destiny through "communication and struggle" (SZ: 384). *Historie* is organized research into past events. English lacks a clear distinction between these concepts (as does French; GA91, 1955: 458). But we can use "history" for *Geschichte* and "historiography" (in a broad sense) for *Historie*. A community may or may not develop historiography, but it cannot help being historical; we inevitably, though often unwittingly, participate in this movement. In turn, a highly historiographical culture may fail to engage with its own historicity in an authentic way.

Authentic historicity focuses primarily on the future, which reveals what has been as a source of possibilities (SZ: 385). This idea persists into Heidegger's late thought.

> As long as we represent history historiographically, it appears as a happening ... in the sequence of before and after. We find ourselves in the present [*Gegenwart*] through which the happening flows. This point of view calculates what is bygone in terms of what is in the present, and plans what is in the future for what is in the present. [This] prevents us from experiencing how authentic history is always the awaiting-toward [*Gegenwart*] ... What presently awaits-toward us, coming toward us, is the future, the coming-to [*Zu-kunft*] ... If the saying "there is nothing new under the sun" means that there is only the old in the inexhaustible transformative power of the inceptive, then the saying hits upon the essence of history. History is the arrival of what has been. (GA79, 1957: 83)

Sometimes, particularly in his middle phase, Heidegger denounces historiography as superficial. The facts established by historians and journalists are "gray scum" (GA95, 1938–39: 96) or "frayed threads of the fluttering semblance of concealed history" (GA96, 1939–41: 250). This attitude exacerbates his political misjudgments and failures of empathy (Polt, 2019: 175–82).

But his fundamental point is sound: Historiographical facts, as significant as they may be, presuppose a fundamentally historical *engagement* that characterizes us whether or not we research the past. Like Hegel's philosophy as the owl of Minerva, historiography may pretend to "paint its gray on gray" in sober detachment from the completed movements of history, but in fact, the very pursuit of historiography is a form of engagement, witting or unwitting, possible only for beings who still have an open future.

Heidegger's conception of history – both human historicity and the history of being – recalls Nietzsche's "On the Advantage and Disadvantage of History for Life" (cf. SZ: 396; GA46, 1938–39). In Nietzsche's terms (1980: 14–18), Heidegger advocates a "monumental" approach to the past, retrieving it as a source of possibilities. But to set the possibilities free from deadening tradition, he also needs a "critical" approach (1980: 21–22). In contrast, "antiquarian" historiography preserves the bygone simply as bygone. As Nietzsche argues (1980: 19–21), antiquarianism sometimes serves a vital purpose (helping us cherish our roots), but all too often it becomes dead weight. And since our past was itself historical – appropriating what we had been for the sake of who we might be – merely antiquarian documentation does not even succeed in genuinely preserving the past.

Since being requires Dasein, in a sense "being happens as the history of humanity, as the history of a people" (GA34, 1931–32: 145). But the history of being is not simply human history. "*Da-sein* is historical only because [history is] essentially and properly the grounding of the truth of beyng as appropriation" (GA69, 1938–40: 94). The engagement at issue in the history of being is not just our own appropriation of who we have been; we are engaged, appropriated, by the very happening of being.

I have used the word "happening" to describe the history of being, just as *Being and Time* uses *Geschehen* for how *Geschichte* occurs (SZ: 375), and Heidegger frequently speaks of *Seinsgeschehnis* in the 1930s. But his later thought is allergic to this term. "In appropriation, nothing happens" (GA97, late 1940s: 382). *Seinsgeschichte* "has nothing to do with a process of happening" (GA91, 1955: 458). I would emphasize the word "process" here. Like its synonym *Vorgang* in an early lecture course (GA56/57, 1919: 75–76), a *Prozeß* is a parade we watch as bystanders, a procession of entities that enter and exit presence in "the sequence of before and after" (GA79, 1957: 83). Happening in a deeper sense *grips* us.

But it also abandons us: The happening of being yields "epochs of presence" (GA91: 663), where "epoch" means holding back (*epochē*). The source of presence remains in darkness. "Metaphysics ... is the history of the self-withdrawal of what sends in favor of the sendings ... of a particular letting-presence of what is present" (GA14, 1962: 50/41). "The expression 'history of being' says that the still concealed event [*Ereignis*] of the difference [between being and beings] sends what is present into presence (then the oblivion of the difference takes place)" (GA83, 1950–51: 220). "The oblivion of being" is not "a defect, an omission," but "the destiny of the clearing of being, for being as presence can become apparent and determine all beings only if the clearing ... holds to itself" (GA13, 1974: 234). We are given presence, but not given an encounter with the *giving* itself – perhaps because what we can encounter is, precisely, what is present. The giving can only be intimated through an experience of the deep contingency of the gift.

Every phase of metaphysics is an answer to an implicit "ontotheological" question (e.g., GA88, 1937–38: 139): What are the general characteristics of what is present, and which entity should be represented as most truly present? (The phrase "metaphysics of presence," which Heidegger never uses, is redundant.) Metaphysics never poses the deeper question: Why does *to be* mean *to be present* in the first place (GA98, 1948–51: 143)? What is the source of the reign of presence? "The history of being begins *with the oblivion of being*" because philosophy "does not think presence precisely as presence, from its truth" (GA5, 1943: 263/196).

What "sends" presence and is thus its "truth" is appropriation. As the "essencing" (*Wesung*) of beyng, appropriation exceeds presencing (*Anwesung*). "Here the essence of beyng is grasped 'historically' ... because now the essence of beyng no longer means only presentness, but the full essencing of the temporal-spatial abyssal ground and thus of truth" (GA65, 1936–38: 2). We must "no longer experience the *transformations of presence* and its clearing in the destiny of letting-be as themselves a [form of] presence" (GA102, 1963: 24). "What appropriation gives, presence, It itself does not *have*; it is not something that presences, it 'is' not at all" (GA102: 44).

Early on, presence is also associated with ground – a questionable and mysterious connection (GA77, 1944–45: 190–91). Philosophy is thus the project of "grounding constant presence" (Schürmann, 1987: 41). "In accordance with each form of presentness, the ground has its character of grounding as ontically causing the actual, as transcendentally making possible the objectivity of objects [Kant], as the dialectical mediation of the movement of absolute spirit [Hegel] or of the historical process of production [Marx], or as the value-positing will to power [Nietzsche]" (GA14, 1964: 70/56).

One can find affinities here between Heidegger and Wittgenstein: Giving reasons and finding grounds makes sense only within an ungrounded language-game or world (Braver, 2012). The appropriating event of grounding the there is abyssal, *ab-gründig* (GA69, 1938–40: 221).

In less densely Heideggerian language: We discover this as the reason for that, but do not question the very search for reasons. We are fascinated by the shine of things, but ignore the invisible event that lets them shine.

A reader in search of that invisible event has to find unspoken, even unthought dimensions of texts. The history of philosophy as usually practiced cannot be enough – because "when the history of beyng is experienced, philosophy has found its end" (GA74: 15/12). Philosophy has operated within the sense of being as presence, unable to reflect on presence itself. So an account that is only faithful to what is directly in a text, no matter how accurate and complete, cannot catch sight of the source of presence. "In order to wrest what the words want to say from what they do say, every interpretation must necessarily use violence" (GA3, 1929: 202).

The happening of being leaves us with presence, but withholds an experience of the event of donation. The tradition cannot understand that presence characterizes its entire understanding of being; but by playing out the iterations of presence, it remains unwittingly loyal to its origin. To deconstruct the tradition, or to have insight into the history of being, is to make presence explicit as what is at work in the shifting difference it makes that there is something instead of nothing. "Guided by the insight that being means presentness," Heidegger dismantles "the tradition that covers [this] up. But it does not just cover up; in it, a transformation of presentness also takes place – in this way, the tradition preserves what is proper to it. Deconstruction [*Destruktion*] is in no case smashing and destruction [*Zerstörung*]" (GA73.2: 1330). Deconstruction reveals presence as a present, a contingent gift – making it possible to appreciate the giving.

But what gives us the right perspective for this operation? Perhaps phenomenology must come first. As Heidegger puts this thought in 1930, his reading of ancient philosophy in terms of being as presence presupposes that human beings "must understand being on the basis of time"; "we cannot spot and find these connections in the ancient conception of being at all unless we have already gotten clear philosophically on the matters at issue" (GA31: 74).

But if the very idea of phenomenology and the idea of philosophy itself (not to mention the idea of an *idea*) are all historical, this order of operations is not correct either. Philosophy as a propaedeutic to reading the great texts is all too naive. Textual interpretation and attention to experience must work hand in hand – so Heidegger blends phenomenology and reading to trace the epochs of presence.

The resulting account shows great continuity over the last forty years of his life. One may suspect he spins a web that reinforces itself without sufficient opportunities for falsification – either challenges from traditional scholarship or attempts such as Derrida's to out-deconstruct the deconstructor. But his thought also leads in various directions that invite further questioning. Here we cannot reach any final judgment on his approach; we can only explain its basic elements and point out some of its fruitful possibilities as well as the riddles it poses.

"What is present can concern humanity according to various ways of presentness. These various ways determine the epochs of the Western history of beyng" (GA79, 1949: 39). Heidegger interprets the epochs in great detail in various texts, but he also provides some concise characterizations of five main epochs.

1. "What is present can essence as what comes forth on its own from concealment into unconcealment" (GA79: 39). This is the Greek experience of *physis*, emergence into the open. For the Greeks, beings shine in a wondrous "surplus" of presence. Greek thought responds to this experience (GA15, 1969: 331/38).

Later Greek philosophy establishes ontotheology through concepts such as Plato's Ideas and Aristotle's *energeia* – the "being at work" that is fully instantiated only in God. Plato is arguably distinct enough from his predecessors that he inaugurates a new epoch. In any case, Plato and Aristotle continue to draw on the experience of *physis*, although no longer in a primordial way; in their thought, the "form" or characteristic presence of entities displaces *physis* as emergence (GA40, 1935: 193/206).

2. The Romans, great engineers and managers, understand presencing in terms of establishing durable results and altering the environment (GA66, 1938–39: 187). Roman philosophy is universally acknowledged to derive from Greek philosophy, so not all readers of Heidegger recognize the Roman era as a distinct epoch. But for Heidegger, the Roman translation of Greek thought is a disaster that has posed obstacles to all later attempts to grasp the Greeks (GA40, 1935: 16/15). Now a thing becomes a *causa*; fulfilled presence degenerates into efficacious activity. "The decisive inflection in the destiny of being as *energeia* lies in its transition to *actualitas*" (GA5, 1946: 371/280). Here, "with one blow the Greek world was toppled" (GA9, 1939: 286/218). (In a jab at the neo-Roman Third Reich, Heidegger cites "the swastika flag flying over the Acropolis" as an instance of this development [GA80.2, 1941: 859].)

3. Medieval monotheism subordinates Roman construction to creation *ex nihilo*, the conversion of absence into presence. "What is present can [then] announce itself as the creation of the Creator, who Himself is constantly and universally present" (GA79, 1949: 39).

4. Modern philosophy shifts focus from the divine mind to the human mind. "What is present can offer itself as what is posited in human representation, for it and counter to it" (GA79: 39) – an object for a conscious subject. "What is, what exists, is only what becomes 'Present' in *cogitatio* as a *cogitatum*. In this character of Presence for *repraesentatio* ... the Greek determination of being, presencing, comes to the fore again, but changed and displaced" (GA80.2, 1941: 866–67).

5. Finally, in our technological age, the subject's representation of objects becomes a global system of manipulation. "What is present can also be as the permanent in the sense of pieces of the standing reserve that, as what is constantly orderable, is set into the positing that holds sway as im-position [*Ge--stell*]" (GA79: 40). Now beings present themselves as resources, always ready to comply with projects of exploitation.

"All interpretation is an overinterpretation" (GA78, 1942: 58; cf. GA96, 1939–41: 211): It steps beyond what is directly present to put it in a new perspective that frees up its potential. Heidegger's interpretation of the epochs of being steps beyond incontrovertible evidence. How could it be otherwise? If we are trying to grasp an experience that was not adequately conceived by those who experienced it (and surely such experiences often happen), we have to venture beyond their words. This venture is necessarily contestable, but it may provide a perspective that unifies seemingly disparate pieces of evidence. It will not be possible to certify Heidegger's perspective as correct, but perhaps it is not arbitrary. In what follows, I limit myself to a few points and questions regarding the beginning and the end of the history of being: Greek thought and modernity, which culminates in technology.

5.2 The Greeks in the History of Being

Is it an arbitrary preconception to say that being means, from antiquity onward, presence – and that what *is* means what presences? (GA73.2: 984)

The Song of Seikilos may be the oldest song to have survived in full, including both lyrics and melody. It is inscribed on a memorial column that dates to the second century AD. The lyrics run: ὅσον ζῇς, φαίνου / μηδὲν ὅλως σὺ λυποῦ / πρὸς ὀλίγον ἔστι τὸ ζῆν / τὸ τέλος ὁ χρόνος ἀπαιτεῖ. "As long as you live, *phainou* / do not grieve at all / living is for a little while / time demands the end." The sense of *phainou*, a middle-voiced imperative form of *phainō*, has puzzled classicists (Rohland, 2023: 2n). But from a Heideggerian point of view, it makes perfect sense. Since you're alive, show yourself: fulfill yourself, realize yourself, shine, radiate. The admonition *phainou* associates presence with life so naturally that it is almost a tautology: Now that you've shown up in this world, *show up!* In its straightforward, economical way, the little verse expresses the importance of *presencing* as an ongoing happening and activity rather than a static *presentness*. It conveys the Greek meaning of being: To be is to *come to presence*.

Or does it? There is no explicit pronouncement on presence or being in the inscription, no theoretical ontology. The word *phainou* might be read politically and ethically: Rather than hiding in fear, be proud and "out." Or one can take it as an eccentric way to express the familiar thought: Seize the day, "eat, drink and be merry" (Rohland, 2023: 2).

The question is whether an interpretive standpoint brings out formerly obscure connections. In my view, the concept of being as presence does prove fruitful in reading a range of texts, both ancient and modern, philosophical and other. It should not eclipse dimensions that Heidegger neglects, but it does provide depth to much that we might otherwise pass over – such as the many forms of *phainō* sprinkled through Greek texts.

Relatively late though the Song of Seikilos is, it harmonizes with much earlier sources. In the fragmentary, possibly Pindaric *Paean* XX, the newborn

Heracles μελέων ἄπο ποικίλον / [σπά]ργανον ἔρριψεν ἐάν τ'ἔφανεν φυὰν: "he flung the decorated swaddling band from his limbs, disclosed his nature" – or, as a translator explains, revealed his "physique" – and killed the attacking serpents (Rutherford, 2001: 401). In more Heideggerian terms, Heracles disclosed his being, brought it into presence. In Pindar, *phya* (a variant of *physis*) "means what one originally and authentically already is: what essences as having been [*das Ge-Wesende*]" (GA40, 1935: 108/111). Heracles' first act is the prototype for his life of heroic feats. If *physis* also means presencing, *ephanen phyan* is a double disclosure: Infant Heracles' own way of presencing came to presence in his deeds. Again, to live in full is to show oneself.

One can also be unconcealed as failing to comprehend unconcealment, as in Pindar's *Nemean Ode* IV.30–32: ἀπειρομάχας ἐών κε φανείη / λόγον ὁ μὴ συνιείς: ἐπεὶ / "ῥέζοντά τι καὶ παθεῖν ἔοικεν." "One would show oneself to be untested in battle if one did not grasp the saying 'the doer is also likely to suffer.'" The thought here is that in war (and life) acts rebound upon the agent; failing to grasp this *logos* reveals (*phaneiē*) one's own being (*eōn*) inexperienced. This showing is not semblance, but being as presencing: The disclosure of someone as naive, as one to whom the truth of one's own life has *not* yet been disclosed, is not yet present.

Presencing can invite errancy, as in Pindar's *Pythian Ode* III.54–55: ἀλλὰ κέρδει καὶ σοφία δέδεται. / ἔτραπεν καὶ κεῖνον ἀγάνορι μισθῷ χρυσὸς ἐν χερσὶν φανείς. "But even wisdom is enchained by profit. Gold shining [*phaneis*] in his hands turned even that man, for a handsome price." In this poem, one who has the art of healing – one to whom ways of making health present have been presented – is tempted by the gleam of gold to commit the hubris of bringing a man back from the dead, and promptly receives capital punishment from Zeus. Although the gold distracts the healer from the greater truth, its brilliance is no illusion but the genuine presencing of an intensely present thing. Maybe those who prize wisdom are *especially* distracted by shining beauty. Heidegger comments (referring to Pindar's *Isthmian Ode* V):

> If *on* [what *is*] means what is present in its presence, then gold as what gleams and shines is more present than other such things ... If gold is more in being than anything else, then being-an-entity [*Seiendsein*] lies in its pure brilliance, which takes place in the gleaming of gold. But brilliance is bringing itself to presencing as what comes out from itself and rests in itself. Shining is presence. (GA78, 1942: 68)

One could indefinitely multiply examples in which presencing seems to be at work in Greek poetic texts. But when we look for confirmation that being means presence in *philosophical* texts, we are faced with the difficulty that although the Greeks took being as presence, "they were far from understanding what this really means" (GA21, 1925–26: 193). There are many occasions for Heidegger to discern unconcealment and presence in Greek philosophy (we cannot come close to reviewing them all), but there is a general hermeneutic problem. "*That* unconcealment is presencing . . . remains outside Greek thinking"; the interpretation of truth as presencing is "*un-Greek* in the sense that through this interpretation, what is Greek – what is inceptive in the thinking of being – first becomes *thinkable* as something handed over to us" (GA66, 1938–39: 316).

So we will find no explicit comprehension of being as presence in Greek thinkers. Nevertheless, Heidegger claims he can determine that their key word *ousia* (traditionally translated as substance or essence, more literally "beingness") is equivalent to *parousia* (presence) (GA21, 1925–26: 193; SZ: 25–26; GA34, 1931–32: 51). His thesis is that although the Greeks contrast *parousia* to *apousia*, presence to absence, these are not just instances of a more general and neutral *ousia*, a beingness that transcends presence and absence. Instead, *ousia* means presence in a more fundamental sense. (In a phenomenological register, compare his statements on *Praesenz* at GA24, 1927: 433.)

A lecture course of 1930 offers one of Heidegger's most thorough arguments for this thesis. He begins with the pre-philosophical meaning of *ousia* as property that we discussed in Section 4.1. "*Ousia* means an entity, but not just any entity: rather, what is *outstanding in its being* in a certain way, that entity that *belongs* to one, possessions and goods, house and home (property, assets), what is available . . . because it *lies safe and undisturbed, constantly available*, at hand" (GA31: 51). *Ousia* "lies nearby, presented on a platter [*auf dem Präsentierteller*]; it *constantly presents itself* . . . it is emphatically *at hand*, in the present, *present*. [Likewise,] we call house and home, assets – what the Greeks designated with *ousia* – *Anwesen*" (GA31: 52).

But everyday usage is only an initial clue to what *ousia* means philosophically (GA31: 54). Heidegger must show that presence is at least implied, and sometimes mentioned, in ancient philosophical accounts of being. He warns us that it is not "enough, wherever expressions and terms come up that concern being, simply to substitute the meaning 'constant presentness'" (GA31: 65). He also cautions that his thesis cannot be proved "by appealing to what is directly and explicitly *meant* in the use of the word" *ousia* (GA31: 60). Nevertheless, he detects presence in six contexts in which Greek philosophers speak of being.

1. Aristotle's analysis of *change* refers explicitly to the presence and absence of opposites (GA31: 60; *Physics* I.7). Presence and absence, *parousia* and *apousia*, mean remaining and not remaining. Thus the core concept of *ousia* is remaining. But remaining means "maintaining constant presentness; beingness, *ousia*, is understood as constant presentness" (GA31: 61).

2. In ancient discussions of *how* things are, disregarding how they change, presence is also at stake, sometimes explicitly. For instance, in Plato's *Euthydemus* (300e–301a), Socrates proposes that beauty "is present" (*parestin*) with beautiful things. As the dialogue shows, the meaning of this expression is puzzling. This indicates that for the Greeks, being means presence in some sense they cannot explain (GA31: 63–64).

3. The Greeks tend to think of being as *substantiality*. A substance or substrate (*hypokeimenon*) is what continues to lie beneath changes; "thus, *in the innermost content of the concept of substance there lies the character of sustained remaining, i.e. constant presentness*" (GA31: 66).

4. What about *existence* or *actuality* – "being versus nonbeing, as in 'to be or not to be, that is the question'" (GA31: 67)? "Actuality" is the degenerate Roman version of *energeia*, which Aristotle associates precisely with *parousia* in his account of change (while *apousia* is associated with *dynamis*, potency) (GA31: 68). Furthermore, the *ergon* or "work" in *energeia* is understood by the Greeks in terms of completion or producedness. To be produced is to be brought forth, to "*stand there*," to be present (GA31: 69; cf. GA66, 1938–39: 187, 195, 289). "*Actuality means producedness, standing-there-ness*" (GA31: 71). *Energeia* is "the presencing of the particular 'this here' ... the lingering of what has been produced, which stands there in its completion" (GA80.2: 859).

5. For Plato, being especially means essence, or *what* an entity is. "What something is, is shown in its 'look,'" its *idea* or *eidos*, "in which the entity presents itself, *is present*" (GA31: 72).

6. To say something *is* is to affirm it is *true*: Being means truth (GA31: 75). Aristotle even calls this the "most eminent" sense of being (*Met.* IX.10). For the Greeks, truth is not primarily a characteristic of thoughts or assertions, but the uncoveredness of beings themselves (GA31: 90). "Unconcealment is the openness of something in such a way that it can present itself on its own. The unconcealment of the simple is simply its own presentness ... *this most constant and purest presentness is nothing other than the highest and most authentic being*" (GA31: 102).

All these arguments can be elaborated and applied to many other texts, as Heidegger does elsewhere (e.g., GA71, 1941–42: 9–72). But let's notice some of their difficulties.

Arguments 1 and 3 rely on the importance of stability or endurance for Greek thinkers. Clearly, they usually see what endures as essential or fundamental; the Eleatics even absolutize permanence. But why should we describe endurance as constant *presence*? This move seems obvious only if we already accept that being is equivalent to presence – but this is precisely what Heidegger claims should *not* be obvious. The move from stability to presence is still more questionable when we recall that he also recognizes a broad sense of presence that includes becoming.

Argument 2 is also problematic. As Heidegger acknowledges, the *Euthydemus* challenges the sense and adequacy of the thought that forms are "present" in individuals. The relation between forms and individuals is more typically described in Plato as resemblance or participation – more concepts that are subjected to severe criticism in the *Parmenides*. Why would one dubious concept, presence, have special significance?

Argument 4 emphasizes the completed product, the *ergon* in the sense of a finished work; but *ergon* also means *working*, an activity, as when Aristotle speaks of the distinctive human *ergon* (*Nic. Eth.* I.7). In fact, the purest activities, such as seeing and thinking, are precisely *not* for the sake of a product; their completion is their very performance (*Met.* IX.6). Here we are far from the everyday sense of *ousia* as possessions. Furthermore, interpreting production as bringing into *presence* is begging the question.

To what extent does argument 6 rely on the etymology of *alētheia*? Remarkably, although Greek philosophers intimately associate being with truth, they nowhere comment on *alētheia* as "unconcealment." Thus, "unconcealment is what is most concealed in Greek Dasein," even though "it determines all presence of what is present from early on" (GA5, 1935–36: 38/28). In the *Cratylus* (421b), Plato introduces a quasi-Heraclitean pseudo-etymology: *alētheia* is *theia alē*, divine wandering. Heidegger comments that truth "is playfully twisted into its very opposite, as opposed to having [something] there uncovered" (GA19, 1924–25: 619). But wandering is the opposite of stability – not of uncovering or presence. Only by thinking of presence as *constant* presence can Heidegger find it indirectly implied in the *Cratylus* – and again, he does not always insist on this narrow sense of presence. Unconcealment is a concept that he *brings* to the ancient texts. This is not to say that his perspective is mistaken, but that it cannot be justified on simply textual grounds.

These points are not refutations, but invitations to more reflection. Again, if the goal is to think what remained unthought (and it would be absurd to hold that thinkers such as Plato and Aristotle, who raise a wealth of unresolved questions, left nothing unthought), we have to go beyond what is directly in the texts. Our motive must ultimately be a *dissatisfaction* that we do not get from our reading, but bring to it.

Heidegger's argument 5 rests on more solid philological ground than the others. The words *idea* and *eidos* are both formed from a verb for seeing, *idein*. Although Plato expressly places the forms in the realm of what is *not* visible but intelligible, he conceives of that realm by analogy to the visible (*Republic*

507b–509a). So there does seem to be an essential element of manifestation, or presence, in the concept of the forms, which are taken as what is most in being and are, as it were, seen with the mind's eye. "These looks are that within which the particular thing *presents* itself as this or that and is *present*" (GA34, 1931–32: 51). The ideal of full clarity, full presence, that is expressed in the theory of forms begins early in Western philosophy and persists through most of it. Parmenides bases his conception of being on "the sheer perception of something at hand in its pure at-handness" (SZ: 25); "being is what shows itself in pure intuitive perception ... original and genuine truth lies in pure intuition. This thesis remains the foundation of Western philosophy from then on" (SZ: 171). Resistance to this ideal motivates many of Heidegger's deconstructive efforts.

Heidegger finds particularly creative accounts of presence in some texts of Plato and Aristotle, and perhaps these accounts point beyond presence itself. In Plato's *Sophist*, "the presentness of what *is not* becomes Present and evident for the first time" (GA19, 1924–25: 193). Heidegger's seminar on Plato's *Parmenides* proposes that "What is most true is when seeming and not-being are taken up into truth and being."[1]

Does this say that Plato enriches presence? Or, as Francisco Gonzalez puts it, that Plato "deliberately seeks to destroy" the supremacy of presence itself "and explicitly defends and develops a radically different conception" (2019: 336)? The *exaiphnēs* or "sudden instant" in the *Parmenides* (156d–e) then anticipates Heidegger by pointing to "a radically different kind of temporality" from the Greek norm (Gonzalez, 2019: 327). Heidegger certainly celebrates the "moment" (SZ: 338), even the "sudden moment" (GA66, 1938–39: 113). His seminar glosses Plato with the claim, "Time is *not* eternity but the moment" (1930–31: 15). But elsewhere he takes the *exaiphnēs* as a form of presence, even a gleam of eternity: "the presence that *essences in itself*; eternity; the *exaiphnēs* (*Parmenides* dialogue)" (GA73.1: 86). Perhaps the root question here is whether "eternity" should be understood as atemporality – a standing now – or as a new, Heideggerian notion in which "the essence of the eternal can be nothing but the deepest sweep *of time*" (GA95, 1938–39: 120). In any case, as suggestive as Plato's concept may be, it is hard to take it as more than an intimation of Heideggerian time, a concept that pushes against the limits of Greek thought without transcending them.

As for Aristotle, he defends the being of potency (*dynamis*) against the Megarians, who argued that only the fully actual can *be*. He conceives of "an entity as there *dynamei* [potentially], present, there now in this way of being"

---

[1] Heidegger, *Plato: Parmenides* (1930–31), unpublished transcript by Herbert Marcuse, Goethe University Frankfurt, University Library Johann Christian Senckenberg, Herbert Marcuse archives, 24.

(GA18, 1924: 380). He "asks about the being-in-the-present of an entity that is there with others and in itself is *dynaton* [potent]" (GA18: 393). For instance, in a runner ready to race, there is an actuality of potency, an "actual presence" of "readiness." Heidegger goes so far as to call this "the greatest philosophical insight of the ancient world, an insight that has remained unappreciated and misunderstood in philosophy to this day" (GA33, 1931: 219).

According to Sean Kirkland, this insight is so radical as to overturn the hegemony of presence: "even if Aristotle will ultimately subordinate *dunamis* to *energeia*, at least he grants it ontological legitimacy, which is more, much more, than the subsequent tradition and its metaphysics of presence will grant to merely potential being" (Kirkland, 2023: 100). Aristotle indicates "the participation *in Being* of non-presence" (Kirkland, 2023: 102). The difficulty with this reading is that Heidegger describes Aristotelian potency precisely as a way of being *present*. Heidegger praises Aristotle for seeing that "the essence of presentness must be understood more fully and flexibly" than in Megarianism (GA33: 184); nevertheless, "Aristotle and the Megarians are completely in agreement on what actuality in general, the being-at-hand of something, means: it means 'the presentness of something'" (GA33: 179). One would also need to consider all the conceptions of power and energy in medieval and modern philosophy and science: The tradition hardly ignores potentiality. Nevertheless, Heidegger does claim that Aristotle brushed up against a new thought – which would presumably set possibility above actuality (SZ: 38).

Of course, Heidegger's readings of Plato and Aristotle may be biased; he may be reading presence into texts that do not mention it at all (Gonzalez, 2006). Then again, as we have seen, if presence is the unspoken presupposition of all Greek thought, a certain amount of "reading into" is required. The danger is that we will fall into a self-confirming interpretation that blinds us to what the texts are genuinely showing us.

Let's turn to the more capacious notion of presence as "presencing" that Heidegger develops in his interpretations of the ancients in the 1940s, especially in his readings of Anaximander. His first interpretation of this pre-Socratic thinker emphasizes that "in and behind presentness stands absentness" (GA35, 1932: 232). GA78 (1942) develops an extensive meditation on Anaximander's few surviving words, which Heidegger condensed into an essay in 1946 and later included in GA5.

For Juan Pablo Hernández, Heidegger's interpretation of Anaximander is the turning point between his early critique of presence and his later acceptance of a rich sense of presencing as the meaning of being. Presence is adequate as long as it is enriched by phenomena traditionally considered absent, such as past and future (Hernández, 2011: 232, 237). One reason to doubt this point is that, as we have seen, Heidegger already entertains the inclusion of absence in presence as early as 1924 (GA18: 376) – soon after the "thunderbolt" in which he initially thought of being as presence, and early in a period that is obviously critical of the tradition. But this does not settle the question of whether, through his creative encounter with Anaximander, Heidegger comes to embrace being as presence. Certainly, his reading is more "monumental" than "critical": It finds *possibilities* in the ancient text.

Let's consider a few highlights of this reading – disregarding exactly how Heidegger bases it on Anaximander's scanty Greek. (Again, his interpretation is very much an "overinterpretation.")

Heidegger proposes that in Anaximander, beings are prototypically "'those that are presently in the present' [*die gegenwärtig Gegenwärtigen*]." But he uses the expression "those that presence" (*die Anwesenden*) to extend presence to past and future beings. These are absent in the present time, yet "present at the time" when they belong (GA78, 1942: 58). The absent "remains essentially tied to what is presently present ... Even the absent is present, and presences into unconcealment *as* what is absent from it" (GA5, 1946: 347).

This is one example of how presence can incorporate absence. "The mode of absence changes in many ways, in accordance with what is present in each case ... In the beginning of presence, absence holds sway": Anaximander's primal *apeiron*, the unlimited, is present precisely through the absence of limits (GA78, 1942: 229).

Broad presence (*Anwesen*) exceeds the narrow present (*Gegenwart*) and is even a condition for it. "The present, in the sense of the present for us, presupposes presentness, and that means 'presence at the time.' Only what presences can come into the present [*gegenwärtig werden*], and only what is in the present can become an object" (GA78: 59). So the presence of an object to a subject is a doubly derivative phenomenon: Primordially there is a present entity, then its appearance in our time, and then our observation of it.

Heidegger asks whether the Greeks reflected on "that into which 'what is' presences as what is present" (GA78: 59). Beings presence into a *time* – not just a point on a timeline, but the site in which presence occurs. This "time-space" is "the open expanse [that] belongs neither to the things that are nor to the humans that are. Both belong to it in different ways" (GA78: 170). This is the clearing or region (*Gegend*) in which we can encounter (*entgegnen*) what is (GA78: 257).

What is presence, then? Not "the empty, pallid property of a 'presentness in general'" but a shining offering. "What is present [is] splendor: what gleams – what offers itself in the gleaming" (GA78: 61). As beings shine, showing up in their abundance, they engage in different measures and modes of presencing, so that "one thing can 'be' presencing more than another" (GA78: 63).

What presences comes forth and passes away; presencing is arrival and departure, origination and destruction (GA78: 120, 135). "Presence is neither mere standing nor mere going," but lingering for a while, staying for an allotted spell (GA78: 175), a fitting time (GA78: 198). But this stay can become a stubborn insistence on staying. Then "presence changes into remaining, into the persistence of what is ever more enduring, that is, the everlasting" (GA78: 176).

What takes part in presencing? All that comes forth as distinct from the human, all that surrounds and faces us as "nature" – but also everything human. Everything that *is* engages in *physis* as "arising from itself" (GA78: 145).

We humans are addressed by the presencing of what presences, solicited by it, destined to be present with it in the shining present. "'Being-there' means presencing in a cleared way to all that is presencing. But this presence that is marked out by the destiny of being does not essence unless the one who is sent by destiny sends himself – that is, unless he himself takes over the task of taking up such presence" (GA78: 92). The destiny or need that governs this relationship between the human and presence is *Brauch*, "requirement" (GA78: 163).

In less Heideggerian words: Being as presencing is the manifestation of things in their fitting locations and moments, and we are responsible for responding to that manifestation appropriately at the time and place where we find ourselves. This response may take the form of art, action, or thought.

This account of being resonates with many of Heidegger's own key themes, such as "time-space" and the "turn," or mutual belonging between Dasein and beyng, in GA65 (1936–38). So is he now accepting that being is presence? Even when he reads Anaximander in the most dedicated and eloquent way, he may be trying to do justice to early Greek thinking without adopting it himself. For example, when he says "even the absent is present," his point may be that presence has such power at the inception of our tradition that it retains the upper hand over absence, dominating and distorting the absent – right down to the concept "absent," which is conceived in terms of presence.

Heidegger's interpretation of *physis* has been celebrated as the understanding of being that he himself is adopting (Capobianco, 2022: 97–98). *Physis* is "growth" as developing and arising (cf. Aristotle, *Met.* V.4). It is "coming forth and coming up, self-opening" (GA4, 1939: 56/79). It is "the emerging and abiding sway" (GA40, 1935: 16/16). But this is precisely "*presencing* in the sense of coming forth into the unconcealed, placing itself into the open" (GA9, 1939: 272/208). And this is what, for the Greeks, all beings do, including humans and gods: "they appear and they presence, they decay and disappear, they look into the unconcealed and they withdraw" (GA55, 1944: 205). Does Heidegger's account of *physis* as presencing name "the temporal and dynamic character of being itself" (Capobianco, 2021: 603), or is his reading only a rich and appreciative interpretation of the Greek conception of being, which is still subject to critique?

Certainly, Heidegger discovers a "presencing" that is richer than "presentness," and one may be attracted to this vision of dynamic flux, emergence and submergence. But then, to be clear, one is not departing from the Greek sense of being. After all, most Greek thinkers fight against the Parmenidean concept of being as full presence in an eternal now. Granted, they typically do so while appealing to some presence that persists through change: the *logos*, the forms, the substrate, elements, atoms, forces, or the divine Mind. But even an extreme theory of total and constant becoming would be motivated by an insistence on presence – the instantaneous, unmistakable presence of a perception (Plato, *Theaetetus* 160c–d). In short, rebellion against permanence neither is un-Greek nor necessarily questions the priority of presence.

So does Heidegger end up in neo-Hellenism? Is he reviving and embracing presence as the meaning of being? His account of *physis* is an appealing vision – but there is evidence from both his middle and his late periods that it is not his core concern.

"'Physics' determines the essence and history of metaphysics from the start," because metaphysics descends from the original experience of being as *physis* or presencing; "but the question of being as such has another essence and another provenance" (GA40, 1953: 20/20). Heidegger seeks "the disclosure of the *essence* of beyng, as opposed to 'physics' up to now" (GA82, 1936: 102). This project is "meta-physical" in the sense that "it no longer has *physis* and *alētheia* as its ground and determination" (GA82, 1936: 135). He also rejects the idea that he intends to introduce a "dynamic" notion of being (GA73.1: 87).

Instead, Heidegger investigates the *source* of the understanding of being as presencing, the *donation* of presencing as the sense of beingness. This source can be called *Seyn* or *Ereignis*, and he clearly distinguishes it from presencing. *Physis* is, "due to the predominance of presencing, the disguising of the abyssal ground of beyng" (GA66, 1938–39: 95–96). "Ap-propriating ... is not presencing into the unconcealed (*physis*)" (GA74: 21/17). "Beyng is not just emergent presencing, but a-byssal appropriating" (GA74: 30/25).

Even though presencing is an event of emergence – the emergence of *beings* – it is not the event of the emergence of *beingness*.

This means that Heidegger's theme of being and time "points to a completely different domain of questioning" from Greek thought (GA40, 1935: 214/229). Likewise, "with *Ereignis*, one is no longer thinking in a Greek way at all" (GA15, 1969: 366/61). What Heidegger wants is "not *flight* into the *Greek* world, but the clear pain of the tearing of the *departure* ... We will never again, and in no form, become '*more Greek* from day to day,' as Nietzsche thinks"

(GA82, 1943: 366). "Only in a thinking that is marked [*bestimmt*] in a Greek way, but is not Greek anymore, does the inceptive saying of being become retrievable for us again" (GA91: 718).

Even "the inception of Western thinking" is unable to grasp presence as such (GA5, 1943: 263/196), so a return to early Greek thought is insufficient.

> The "ambivalence" in the thinking of the pre-Socratics is to be understood as meaning that they did not yet properly think being in the ontological difference. This "not yet" creates the impression that they were already thinking beyond metaphysics, as it were – thinking being as such. This "not yet" suggests the possibility of elucidating the question of being as such through the thinking of the pre-Socratics, in conversation with them, that is, to attribute [*unterzulegen*] something that is no longer Greek to them in one's interpretation [*Auslegen*] ... The "not yet" as prehistory is something other than the "no longer" after the "overcoming of metaphysics." (Heidegger, 1964: 217)

These texts leave no room for doubt that Heidegger's goal is not to revive the early Greek understanding of being as presencing, no matter how sympathetically he elucidates it in some texts. A singular historical moment cannot be relived; to retrieve it can only mean to confront it in order to gain an impetus for our *own* future. In fact, as Taylor Carman observes, "that Heidegger did not himself embrace the ontology of the Presocratics is clear from his own account of Dasein as fundamentally futural": we are not "things dawning and lingering in the world, but ... agents interpreting themselves and their situation by projecting into possibilities" (1995: 438).

Heidegger insists that although the Greeks were immersed in presence, "presence did *not* become *worthy* of question for them *as* the presence *of* what is present" (GA8, 1952: 241/238). "Greek philosophy never went back into [presence as the] ground of being, into what it harbors. It remained in the foreground of what is present" (GA40, 1935: 65/66). "If we understand *ousia* as presencing ... for whom and where does this presence presence? That is, in what timespace in the broadest sense? It is strange and highly significant that this question, as a question, does not arise among the Greeks" (GA83, 1944: 459).

This non-Greek inquiry into the source and site of the understanding of being is Heidegger's pursuit.

5.3 Modernity in the History of Being

Far more could be said about Heidegger's interpretation of the Greeks. But we will now set it aside, skip his accounts of the Roman and medieval epochs, and turn to his account of modernity – an epoch in which we still stand, in a technological phase whose cybernetic development Heidegger foresaw.

Heidegger traces the following line from the ancients to the moderns: presencing – presentness – permanence – objectivity – certainty (GA70, 1941: 63/48). With Descartes, the turn to objectivity and certainty is complete: the presence of what is present takes the form of "Presence in *repraesentatio*" (GA5, 1938: 110/84). In turn, thinking becomes the "presentation of the Present" (GA7, 1952: 141). In self-consciousness, Descartes discovers "what is indubitable because it is constantly presencing in every *cogitatio*" (GA86, 1942–43: 727).

With Hegel, we have the apotheosis of this form of presence: His absolute is "the present that is in the present for itself, presentness reflecting itself in presencing" (GA68, 1938–39, 32).

With Nietzsche, presence takes the form of "constant creation and destruction" (GA44, 1937: 227), perpetual becoming (GA47, 1939: 271), eternal "overpowering ... the making-constant of presencing without a goal, without unconditional fixation, the presencing of non-subsistence as such" (GA67, 1938–39: 45).

With this, we reach the epoch that Heidegger most famously describes in "The Question Concerning Technology" (GA7, 1953). Since this is his own age and ours, it is of special importance if we are to feel the dissatisfaction that can drive us to critique the tradition of being as presence and set free different possibilities.

Now the phenomenon of "standing reserve" or "resources" (*Bestand*) "characterizes nothing less than the way in which everything presences, everything that is touched by the challenging unconcealing" (GA7, 1953: 17/17). All that *is* now appears as material to be extracted or exploited for energy, to be grasped (conceptually and practically) by humans in service of the "will to will." The Earth becomes a gigantic gas station (GA16, 1955: 523/MA 50). Heidegger dubs this regime of unconcealment *das Ge-stell*, "enframing" or "im-position": It sets resources in place so they are ready to be set to work, yielding power. "What is present concerns today's humanity as what can be ordered [*das Bestellbare*] in this or that way ... The mode of presence of resources is orderability, characterized by the possibility of the inconstant, the ever new and improved, without any view to what is best" (GA16, 1965: 625/QCD 217).

Im-position is a Procrustean bed: Whatever does not fit seamlessly into the system of resources gets mutilated. Everything has the same meaning. There are no stable objects anymore, just a monotonous flux: "The instability of resources creates the semblance of persistence through the uninterrupted exchange of what has no endurance" (GA100, ca. 1957: 259). There is no more mystery, depth, distance, and especially destiny: no sense of who we are as a mission, a challenge, a question. The question has been answered: We are users and managers. By the same token, we are the used and the managed: "humanity itself has become the ordered resource of setting-to-order" (GA100, 1957: 277). We are human resources.

Heidegger grants that technological devices provide many benefits. But their advantages, along with the profit they generate, are not what he believes drives the technological world view. It is driven by the sheer will to overpower for the sake of overpowering, with no goal beyond itself – just what Nietzsche celebrated. (Again, we cannot discuss whether this is a fair reading of Nietzsche.) The claimed benefits of technical innovation obscure its real motive: It *must* be done because it *can* be done.

For us today, of course, electronic computing is the prime form of "technology." Heidegger lived long enough to predict that cybernetics – defined by Norbert Wiener (1948) as the theory of "control and communication in the animal and the machine" – would become the master science. Not just that, but it is a harbinger of the completion of the history of being as presence:

> Because cybernetics, without knowing it or being able to think it, remains subordinated to this change [from objectivity to orderability] in the presentness of what is present, it [is] only a sign of the end of philosophy. This end itself consists in the fact that with the orderability of what is present, the last possibility in the transformation of presentness has been reached ... The dissolution of philosophy develops into an orderable task whose unity is resolved by the emergence of cybernetics. (GA16, 1965: 626/QCD 217–18)

Heidegger may seem to be prophesying here, or mimicking Hegel. If the donations of epochs of presence are essentially contingent and mysterious, how can we be sure we have reached the end? But there is, at least, an inner logic to modernity that we can understand as leading to the cybernetic age. "We do not know the future [but] insight into the present is enough": "the power of the positing that challenges forth ... sets humanity itself the task of securing everything present, and thus humanity too, in its orderability" (GA16, 1965: 627/QCD 218). For Descartes, the collective human mind can become "masters and possessors of nature" by determining the mathematical laws that govern the motion of objects; then all the forces of the universe can be harnessed to yield "appropriate," that is, feasible, results (*Discourse on Method* VII). The nonquantifiable aspects of beings are to be disregarded or dissolved in the "liquidation of the real" (Polt, 2018). This project requires techniques of data gathering, calculation, and storage, so the need for information technology is built into the Cartesian project.

In the twenty-first century, our world is constantly scanned, measured, and recorded. We inhabit a global positioning system, a quickly spreading and indefinitely extendable regime of tracking and surveillance. Everything, especially including us, is treated as a resource to be datamined, monetized, and controlled. Nothing seems to resist our digital systems of representation. Everything leaves rich trails of information. We are surrounded by ultra-high-definition representations that lay claim to truth and utility. Our attention, desires, and behavior are continually channeled into this system. (Again, think of that sinking feeling when you ask yourself: Where's my phone?)

The accuracy of cybernetic representation depends on oceans of binary data: nanopresences and nanoabsences, ones and zeroes, which are algorithmically processed to yield new ways of producing what is present. This information is "orderable" in two senses: It can be "crunched" into various formations, and it is on call so that we can place orders for desired goods and services. Whenever we take a mobile device from our pocket to schedule the delivery of a product that lies ready in a massive warehouse, we rely on a highly complex and sophisticated system of control and communication, presentation and representation, that uses modern science and technology – and thus is founded on modern philosophy, which in turn would not be possible without a history that reaches back to the primal experience of presencing among the Greeks. That, at least, would be Heidegger's analysis.

What is wrong with this world, from his point of view? Certainly, it fills needs, supplies enjoyment, and brings opportunities. It has also created an ecological catastrophe that looms like a tsunami. But neither this "positive" nor this "negative" are decisive. The deeper catastrophe, for Heidegger, is our indifference to the concealment of being – our obliviousness to the hidden source of the difference it makes that there is something instead of nothing. For us, to *be* is to be a resource subjected to information processing – but why? We have sunk into our current form of unconcealment so deeply that, he fears, there may be no reawakening to the event of the opening of the "there."

In Heidegger's nightmare of technological presence, our very organ of thought will get reduced to a cybernetically managed resource:

> Maybe . . . everything will freeze in machination, and this frozenness will make itself out to be life. Then there would be no more inauthentic oblivion, nor would authentic oblivion arrive; neither would having-been essence, nor would requirement's arrival into releasement take place. Humanity would have gotten what it has been asking for for centuries: the "present" [*"Gegenwart"*] that it takes as being. Humanity would operate . . . in the technical administration of itself and its brain. The preparation and steering of this organ by electric currents, immobilizing some centers and mobilizing others, which would always seem useful, would offer itself as the culmination of all organization. Not by the mass killing of human beings, but by the fact that *Homo americanus* [*der amerikanische Mensch*] will absolutely objectify life = the world, by organizing this organ: this is how humanity will be thrust into the uttermost abjectness of the frozen oblivion of being. (GA97, late 1940s: 308–9)

We have now entered a stage of cybernetics that Heidegger could not quite have envisioned, although he anticipated "the thinking machine" around 1940 (GA96: 195). Automated forms of historiography "scrape" up all available records of human activity. Generative artificial intelligence empowers computers to construct new representations that are often indistinguishable from those made by people. What form of presence is this? It no longer has to be presence to consciousness or will, although a human user may employ the results of AI. Aside from the misuses of AI by malicious agents, and the perhaps far-fetched anxiety that AI itself will set its sights on exterminating its inventors, there is a risk that human thought and art will be overwhelmed by the profusion of machine-generated representations, and that the effort to meditate on meaning will seem meaningless.

It should be clear by now that "How does it stand with presence?" is far from a merely academic question. The cybernetic sense of presence is dangerously narrow in its understanding of being, even as it is dangerously broad in its ambition to embrace all that is.

But "*must* beings be perceived as what *presences* . . . ? If not, why not? . . . If not as 'what presences,' in what other way? What determines the otherness? Destiny?" (GA73.2: 1224).

The alternative Heidegger suggests is, as we saw in Section 4.3, an experience of beings as "things" within the fourfold. Their being will no longer be an epoch of presence, he imagines. This is not to say that things will simply lose the sense of presence – much less that they will be absent. "One day, the way via the representational thinking of beings as such will no longer be necessary; this does not mean that beings will be obliterated – rather, the presence of what is present will first be authentically cleared in the thinging of the thing, and preserved in the world" (GA98, 1948–51: 255). "In the thing, the onetime presence of what is present is saved up" (GA98: 244).

Presence is now brought into its proper context, so that the dimension of *ownness* prevails. As we noted, with a new experience of what *lets* presence take place, "what is present will transform itself into the appropriated – the befitted of the befitting of the fourfold" (GA73.2: 1295). "The thing has not yet been *thought as thing. If it is thought as thing, we will experience world*. From world, everything that is present takes place otherwise" (GA91: 564). "Presence-to is to be thought . . . on the basis of the appropriating event of world. Purely preserved presence takes place in thinging" (GA99, 1947–50: 161).

Heidegger invests a great deal of hope in the fourfold and its "things" – a vision he developed amid the rubble and deprivation of postwar Germany, in the spirit of starting anew with pure and humble elements. It is a vision of a serene and meaningful existence, in which people live with limits and accept their place in a mysterious but coherent world. But how plausible is this vision for a planet that has been transformed by modernity, whose cultures are blending and shifting, where meaning is rushing into unprecedented configurations and unanticipated chasms? He denies that objects can be transformed into things by "a mere change of attitude" or by recollecting "former, old objects that were perhaps once on the way to becoming things, and presencing as things, and determining all presence by thinging" (GA80.2, 1950: 978). "The human being can do nothing" (GA80.2: 973), but can "act" only in the form of thinking (GA80.2: 974). Perhaps, however, local practices that elude the cybernetic regime may let us experience "thinging," or other ways to be that are irreducible to presence.

6 Presence and Engagement

So it all comes to this: the turning point, the crux. I prepare to leap or not to leap. My choice now will irrevocably affect the course and shape of my life – past, present, and future. I see that everything hinges on my movement at this moment, even though I can't make out the details. Is this seeing at all? Or a far deeper perception?
There is no time for that question. The kairos *has arrived.*
My hand reaches out.

"Presence" is an empty word unless we connect it to experience. A text can never do this for us, even if it does not just explicate other texts but tries to put phenomena into words. Words are words, not experiences. It is up to *readers* to bring the text to bear on how things are manifest to them. Then the text becomes a "formal indication": an invitation to supply words with content by deepening one's own way of existing (GA29/30, 1930: 428–31). "Being means presence; what *is* means what presences. To what extent do we experience something definite here? ... Where do we find ourselves pointed when we experience what presences *as* what presences?" (GA73.2: 1249–50)

As we reach the end of this study, I invite readers to reflect on the experience of studying. As we study, as we think, as we practice philosophy, we observe what is manifest. We attend to its current presentation. We try to get clearer on what is present, how it is present, and what else might become present through it. We watch it deploy itself, display itself, unfold. We ourselves try to be present with it, to know it.

But Heidegger asks us to attend not only to what presences, but to presencing itself. Moreover, he wants us to ask what allows presencing to take place, and to experience *that*. What kind of attending is required here? Should it still be called "philosophy"?

That question may just seem to invite us to choose how to use a word. But Heidegger claims that the tradition has already answered: "Philosophy contemplates what presences in its presence" (GA5, 1942–43: 128/96). It does not question "presentness as such" (GA16, 1965: 631/QCD 221). It does not ask what *gives* presence.

With this claim, Heidegger seems to place himself in the line of the masters of the hermeneutics of suspicion: Marx, Nietzsche, Freud. For them, traditional discourse must be diagnosed as a symptom of a ground that it cannot bring itself to speak, but that their analysis reveals: class interests, the will to power, the id. Is *Ereignis* another such postulate? Heidegger would argue that his predecessors have only tried to identify the most present entity and ground. They have not experienced *letting*-presence.

What about phenomenology – the effort to "let what shows itself be seen from itself just as it shows itself from itself" (SZ: 34)? If this concept is so broad that it includes any experience and attitude, any way of attending to the issue in question, then there is nothing to be said against it. But if, despite the richness and variety of phenomenological description, "showing" and "seeing" are bound to presence, then phenomenology is inadequate to Heidegger's project. A *phainomenon*, after all, is precisely what *presents* itself (GA63, 1923: 68; GA17, 1923–24: 9; GA98, ca. 1950: 278). But "what can never appear as something that presences is presentness itself" (GA100, 1952–57: 89).

Can phenomenology, then, address what *lets* presence happen? "How can the characterization of presentness, of presence as *letting presence*, be exhibited phenomenologically?" (GA73.2: 1232).

Heidegger explores "the fate of phenomenology" in several texts (McNeill, 2020). The most unambiguous statements against phenomenology are to be found in the 1936 "Running Notes on *Being and Time*," an agitated text that presents Dasein as a possibility, not a phenomenon. Phenomenology calls for "'intuition of essences'; description; but essence can only be created – not found and researched!" (GA82: 43). Phenomenology does not "question historically" (GA82: 37). The phenomenological frame of *Being and Time* makes it seem to "describe and analyze Da-sein as if it were something at hand" (GA82: 45). Instead, thinking is a venture, an experiment, a leap.

Heidegger's late phrase "a phenomenology of the inapparent" (GA102, ca. 1970: 328; GA15, 1973: 399/80) is more ambiguous. It can be taken either as a harmless expression – since phenomenology never simply describes what is obviously in the foreground – or, more likely, as a paradox that implies that phenomenology inevitably fails to think of what *cannot* appear, *cannot* be present. In his very late notes for an unfinished preface to the *Gesamtausgabe*, he describes the inapparent as "what *holds itself in itself* in all presence" (Heidegger, 2012: 73). It demands not *logos* as explanation, but a special kind of "saying," a "phenomenophasis"

(2012: 76, 82, 84, 87, 89), or even a "tautophasis" – a saying of the selfsame that respects *"withdrawal"* (2012: 71) and the inevitability of concealment (2012: 95).

Perhaps it is best to let the term "phenomenology" "fade away in favor of the matter of thinking, whose openness remains a mystery." The spirit of phenomenology will persist as the possibility of "corresponding to the demand of what is to be thought" (GA14, 1963: 101/82). The "corresponding" here (*Entsprechen*) does not mean asserting a correct theory, but speaking in response to what is at stake. To attend here does not mean to observe what is present at hand, but to tend to what demands our involvement (cf. Berger, 2023). It is waiting upon the issue, devotedly giving it the time it needs to sink in.

What, then, is at issue in presence? This is not just a question about Heidegger, but about our own experience, and about how things make a difference to us now and in the future.

When we focus only on the presence of what is present – even if we understand it broadly – we disregard *engagement*. For early Heidegger, this primarily means engagement in individual temporality: "The question 'What is time?' became 'Who is time?' More closely: Are we ourselves time? Or still more closely: Am I my time?" (GA64, 1924: 125/22E). In his political phase, it means engagement in a shared history: "Who are we?" (GA 36/37, 1933–34: 176). In his late, post-political phase, it means meditative engagement with the destiny bequeathed to humanity: Who may humans become? Throughout, there is an element of belonging and self-transformation that is obscured when we are absorbed in the present.

The call for engagement is there in 1919, when Heidegger distinguishes an objective *Vorgang* from an appropriative *Ereignis* (GA56/57: 75–76). It is there in *Being and Time* when he chooses "care" as the name for our very being. It is there later when he rediscovers *Ereignis* as a name for the grounding of the "there."

These words point to how we engage in, and are engaged by, what calls for attention. To engage is to stake a claim in a matter, to make a commitment, to join battle. But this act presupposes that we have already *been* engaged: We have been been staked, we are burdened with responsibility, we find ourselves in the midst of a battle. Even a newborn has intense experiences of importance, albeit in a narrow range (GA27, 1928–29: 125–26). This prior engagement challenges us to develop abilities, attention, and connections that enrich and deepen our experience. There is a mutual exchange between our being meaningfully engaged and our engaging in meaning. This twofold engagement is always at work, but it can take place more or less intensely and lucidly.

Heidegger wants engagement to intensify. In his middle period he emphasizes activity, in his late period receptivity, but both are always important. At the heart of his critique of the tradition is the idea that philosophy has neglected the essential role of twofold engagement, and has focused instead on what is present within the field of presence that emerges from engagement.

But have no other philosophers understood the priority of engagement? That would be a dubious assertion. In the American philosophical tradition, which Heidegger hardly knew, engagement is a central theme. In his more sympathetic readings, Heidegger himself finds engagement at least suggested in the texts he reads: for example, in Anaximander's *to khreōn*, which he interprets as *Brauch* – the requiring that summons us to attend to being (GA78, 1942: 134–36). If we consider the drama and characterization in Plato's dialogues, we can also discover engagement there: Plato does not just theorize, but portrays the human context that moves individuals to look for what matters. Writers such as Kierkegaard and Nietzsche achieve comparable feats. Of course, such writers may not be concerned with being labeled "philosophers."

In any case, to take things as merely present in their presentness is to forget that the sense of things has always been put at stake along with our own being, in every encounter and every interpretation. The stakes do not directly show up as present. No microscope or telescope reveals them. Hence the illusion of mere data, neutrally available to a neutral mind. Hence the ability to digitize and process information, and to rely on the results as if they captured what is at stake, as if what we see and do exhausted who we are.

Engagement is required if we are to attend to what is present. What is present must first matter to us; it must make a difference. We are essentially receptive to the difference between something and nothing. This difference itself challenges us to seize our own seizedness, to appropriate our appropriation, to *re*-engage. If we neglect this challenge, no amount of description and theorizing will transcend presentness – and thought will be reduced to an assertion that "is passed on in an empty way of understanding, is uprooted, and turns into a free-floating thesis" (SZ: 36). To put this point into pointers:

We make claims as if we were not claimed.
We attend to facts, disregarding our own attendance.
We arrive at conclusions, forgetting our own arrival.
We draw the contours of what is present, neglecting how we have been drawn into presence.
We describe what we witness, ignoring that witnessing is testifying, and that we have been called to the stand.

To recall the calling, the drawing, the arriving, the attending, the claiming – without turning them into yet more facts about what is present: That is the task.

The critique of presence is not yet another theory, but a question of Dasein, of how we are there. "In being-there and *as* being-there, beyng itself becomes *truth* (poetry – work – deed). And only where this happens is there the *need* for philosophy. If there were not this *happening of being* – the ground of our self – then we would not be capable of *cognizing* or *knowing*" (GA73.1: 445). "The *over-coming* of metaphysics has to do with being *there*. It cannot be carried out by publishing a 'book'; what looks like such a 'book' literally has another essence" (GA67, 1938–39: 39).

Have we answered the question: How does it stand with presence?

To the end, Heidegger challenged himself to inquire into presence, not to rest satisfied with a doctrine. Even the most basic issue of the relation between presence and the temporal present remained unresolved: Is it the case that "the present can never be thought on the basis of presentness" (GA73.2: 907), or that "the present is grounded on presence" (GA73.2: 946)? In 1975 he was still asking himself, "Is being present equivalent to being in the present?" (Heidegger, 2012: 54).

So there is no answer. But this means that Heidegger never abandoned his critique of the tradition. Even when he most deeply appreciates the original Greek experience of presencing, he does so with a view to inaugurating a different kind of questioning, which asks about the *granting* of presencing. Even when he accepts presence as our destined and inescapable sense of being, he asks whether presence is *enabled* by a mysterious "event" that lets things come to the fore while it itself keeps quiet. Thinking of this "event" may in turn transform our understanding of things so that they no longer fit any traditional sense of presence.

It may also transform how *we* stand with presence. For Heidegger's "thunderbolt" implies that even if the sum total of information about us could be collected, it would omit the distinctive way in which we make a difference, are engaged in meaning, and are at stake. Facts characterize only what is present – not its presencing as such, nor the source of presencing. Whatever we may call that source, it lies at the heart of who we are – even if it leaves us in the dark, or perhaps precisely because it resists the glare of presence.

"Light is not a clearing anymore if the clear dissolves into mere brightness, 'brighter than a thousand suns'" (GA79, 1957: 93).[2]

---

[2] In his translation, Andrew Mitchell notes that Heidegger quotes the title of Jungk (1958 [German ed. 1956]). Jungk claims (201) that the phrase from the *Bhagavad-Gita* "the radiance of a thousand suns" "flashed into [J. Robert Oppenheimer's] mind" as he witnessed the explosion of the first atomic bomb.

Acknowledgments

I am grateful to Gregory Fried for his many insights into this project. For their comments and questions, I also thank Elena Bartolini, Dana Belu, Benjamin Brewer, Noam Cohen, Patrick Gamez, Jeffrey Gower, Lawrence Hatab, Bethany Henning, Drew Hyland, Rylie Johnson, Mat Messerschmidt, Kevin Miles, Andrew Mitchell, Ian Moore, Douglas Peduti, Robert Pippin, Robert Scharff, and Adriel Trott.

References

Texts by Heidegger

(1964). Letter to Dieter Sinn. Excerpts originally published on kotte-autographs .com, reproduced in D. F. Ferrer (2022), *Martin Heidegger as Interrogator*, self-published.

(1967). *Sein und Zeit*, 11th ed., Tübingen: Max Niemeyer (1st ed. 1927).

(2012). *Auszüge zur Phänomenologie aus dem Manuskript "Vermächtnis der Seinsfrage,"* Jahresgabe der Martin-Heidegger-Gesellschaft 2011/2012, Meßkirch: Martin-Heidegger-Gesellschaft.

Gesamtausgabe, Frankfurt: Vittorio Klostermann, 1976–

Translations are listed only if they include material cited in this study.

GA1 (1978). *Frühe Schriften.*
GA3 (1991). *Kant und das Problem der Metaphysik.*
  (1997) *Kant and the Problem of Metaphysics*, 5th ed., Bloomington: Indiana University Press.
GA4 (1981). *Erläuterungen zu Hölderlins Dichtung.*
  (2000) *Elucidations of Hölderlin's Poetry*, Amherst, NY: Humanity Books.
GA5 (1977). *Holzwege.*
  (2002) *Off the Beaten Track*, Cambridge: Cambridge University Press.
GA6.2 (1997). *Nietzsche II.*
  (1973) *The End of Philosophy*, New York: Harper & Row.
GA7 (2000). *Vorträge und Aufsätze.*
  (1977) *The Question Concerning Technology and Other Essays*, New York: Harper & Row.
GA8 (2002). *Was heißt Denken?*
  (1968) *What Is Called Thinking?* New York: Harper & Row.
GA9 (1976). *Wegmarken.*
  (1998) *Pathmarks*, Cambridge: Cambridge University Press.
GA11 (2006). *Identität und Differenz.*
  (1963) Preface (WJR), in W. J. Richardson, *Heidegger*, New York: Fordham University Press.
  (1969) *Identity and Difference* (ID), New York: Harper & Row.
GA12 (1985). *Unterwegs zur Sprache.*
  (1971) *On the Way to Language*, New York: Harper & Row.

GA13 (1983). *Aus der Erfahrung des Denkens.*
GA14 (2007). *Zur Sache des Denkens.*
  (1972) *On Time and Being*, New York: Harper & Row.
GA15 (1986). *Seminare.*
  (2003) *Four Seminars*, Bloomington: Indiana University Press.
GA16 (2000). *Reden und andere Zeugnisse eines Lebensweges.*
  (1966) Memorial address (MA), in *Discourse on Thinking*, New York: Harper & Row.
  (1990) Martin Heidegger in conversation (MHC), in G. Neske and E. Kettering, eds., *Martin Heidegger and National Socialism*, New York: Paragon.
  (2009) *Der Spiegel* interview with Martin Heidegger (SI), in G. Figal, ed., *The Heidegger Reader*, Bloomington: Indiana University Press.
  (2010) On the question concerning the determination of the matter for thinking (QCD), *Epoché*, 14(2), 213–23.
GA17 (1994). *Einführung in die phänomenologische Forschung.*
  (2005) *Introduction to Phenomenological Research*, Bloomington: Indiana University Press.
GA18 (2002). *Grundbegriffe der aristotelischen Philosophie.*
  (2009) *Basic Concepts of Aristotelian Philosophy*, Bloomington: Indiana University Press.
GA19 (1992). *Platon: Sophistes.*
  (1997) *Plato's "Sophist,"* Bloomington: Indiana University Press.
GA20 (1979). *Prolegomena zur Geschichte des Zeitbegriffs.*
  (1992) *History of the Concept of Time: Prolegomena*, Bloomington: Indiana University Press.
GA21 (1976). *Logik.*
  (2010) *Logic*, Bloomington: Indiana University Press.
GA22 (1993). *Die Grundbegriffe der antiken Philosophie.*
  (1997) *Basic Concepts of Ancient Philosophy*, Bloomington: Indiana University Press.
GA24 (1975). *Die Grundprobleme der Phänomenologie.*
  (1982) *The Basic Problems of Phenomenology*, Bloomington: Indiana University Press.
GA26 (1978). *Metaphysische Anfangsgründe der Logik im Ausgang von Leibniz.*
  (1984) *The Metaphysical Foundations of Logic*, Bloomington: Indiana University Press.
GA27 (1996). *Einleitung in die Philosophie.*
  (2024) *Introduction to Philosophy*, Bloomington: Indiana University Press.

GA29/30 (1983). *Die Grundbegriffe der Metaphysik.*
(1995) *The Fundamental Concepts of Metaphysics*, Bloomington: Indiana University Press.
GA31 (1982). *Vom Wesen der menschlichen Freiheit.*
(2002) *The Essence of Human Freedom*, London: Continuum.
GA33 (1981). *Aristoteles, Metaphysik Θ 1–3.*
(1995) *Aristotle's "Metaphysics" Θ 1–3*, Bloomington: Indiana University Press.
GA34 (1988). *Vom Wesen der Wahrheit.*
(2002) *The Essence of Truth*, London: Continuum.
GA35 (2011). *Der Anfang der abendländischen Philosophie.*
(2015) *The Beginning of Western Philosophy*, Bloomington: Indiana University Press.
GA36/37 (2001). *Sein und Wahrheit.*
(2010) *Being and Truth*, Bloomington: Indiana University Press.
GA38 (1998). *Logik als die Frage nach dem Wesen der Sprache.*
(2009) *Logic as the Question Concerning the Essence of Language*, Albany: State University of New York.
GA40 (1983). *Einführung in die Metaphysik.*
(2014) *Introduction to Metaphysics*, 2nd ed., New Haven, CT: Yale University Press.
GA44 (1986). *Nietzsches metaphysische Grundstellung im abendländischen Denken.*
(1984) *Nietzsche*, vol. 2, San Francisco: Harper & Row.
GA45 (1984). *Grundfragen der Philosophie.*
(1994) *Basic Questions of Philosophy*, Bloomington: Indiana University Press.
GA46 (2003). *Zur Auslegung von Nietzsches II. Unzeitgemäßer Betrachtung.*
(2016) *Interpretation of Nietzsche's Second Untimely Meditation*, Bloomington: Indiana University Press.
GA47 (1989). *Nietzsches Lehre vom Willen zur Macht als Erkenntnis.*
GA48 (1986). *Nietzsche: Der europäische Nihilismus.*
GA49 (1991). *Die Metaphysik des deutschen Idealismus.*
(2021) *The Metaphysics of German Idealism*, London: Polity.
GA50 (1990). *Nietzsches Metaphysik; Einleitung in die Philosophie – Denken und Dichten.*
(2011) *Introduction to Philosophy: Thinking and Poetizing*, Bloomington: Indiana University Press.
GA51 (1981). *Grundbegriffe.*
(1993) *Basic Concepts*, Bloomington: Indiana University Press.

GA52 (1982). *Hölderlins Hymne "Andenken."*
(2018) *Hölderlin's Hymn "Remembrance,"* Bloomington: Indiana University Press.
GA53 (1984). *Hölderlins Hymne "Der Ister."*
(1996) *Hölderlin's Hymn "The Ister,"* Bloomington: Indiana University Press.
GA54 (1982). *Parmenides.*
(1992) *Parmenides*, Bloomington: Indiana University Press.
GA55 (1979). *Heraklit.*
(2018) *Heraclitus*, London: Bloomsbury.
GA56/57 (1987). *Zur Bestimmung der Philosophie.*
(2000) *Towards the Definition of Philosophy*, London: Continuum.
GA58 (1992). *Grundprobleme der Phänomenologie.*
(2013) *Basic Problems of Phenomenology*, London: Continuum.
GA60 (1995). *Phänomenologie des religiösen Lebens.*
(2004) *The Phenomenology of Religious Life*, Bloomington: Indiana University Presss.
GA61 (1985). *Phänomenologische Interpretationen zu Aristoteles.*
(2008) *Phenomenological Interpretations of Aristotle*, Bloomington: Indiana University Press.
GA63 (1988). *Ontologie. Hermeneutik der Faktizität.*
(1999) *Ontology: The Hermeneutics of Facticity*, Bloomington: Indiana University Press.
GA64 (2004). *Der Begriff der Zeit.*
(2011) *The Concept of Time*, London: Continuum, pp. 3–102.
(1992) *The Concept of Time*, Oxford: Blackwell, pp. 107–25.
GA65 (1989). *Beiträge zur Philosophie (Vom Ereignis).*
(2012) *Contributions to Philosophy (Of the Event)*, Bloomington: Indiana University Press.
GA66 (1997). *Besinnung.*
(2006) *Mindfulness*, London: Continuum.
GA67 (1999). *Metaphysik und Nihilismus.*
(2022) *Metaphysics and Nihilism*, Cambridge: Polity.
GA68 (1993). *Hegel.*
(2015) *Hegel*, Bloomington: Indiana University Press.
GA69 (1998). *Die Geschichte des Seyns.*
(2015) *The History of Beyng*, Bloomington: Indiana University Press.
GA70 (2005). *Über den Anfang.*
(2023) *On Inception*, Bloomington: Indiana University Press.

GA71 (2009). *Das Ereignis*.
   (2013) *The Event*, Bloomington: Indiana University Press.
GA73.1, 73.2 (2013). *Zum Ereignis-Denken*.
GA74 (2010). *Zum Wesen der Sprache und Zur Frage nach der Kunst*.
   (2023) *On the Essence of Language and the Question of Art*, Cambridge: Polity.
GA75 (2000). *Zu Hölderlin – Griechenlandreisen*.
GA76 (2009). *Leitgedanken zur Entstehung der Metaphysik, der neuzeitlichen Wissenschaft und der modernen Technik*.
GA77 (1995). *Feldweg-Gespräche*.
   (2010) *Country Path Conversations*, Bloomington: Indiana University Press.
GA78 (2010). *Der Spruch des Anaximander*.
GA79 (1994). *Bremer und Freiburger Vorträge*.
   (2012) *Bremen and Freiburg Lectures*, Bloomington: Indiana University Press.
GA80.2 (2020). *Vorträge. Teil 2: 1932–1967*.
GA82 (2018). *Zu eigenen Veröffentlichungen*.
   (2025) *On My Own Publications*, Bloomington: Indiana University Press.
GA83 (2012). *Seminare: Platon – Aristoteles – Augustinus*.
GA86 (2011). *Seminare: Hegel – Schelling*.
GA88 (2008). *Seminare (Übungen) 1937/38 und 1941/42*.
GA89 (2017). *Zollikoner Seminare*.
   (2001) *Zollikon Seminars*, Evanston, IL: Northwestern University Press.
GA91 (2022). *Ergänzungen und Denksplitter*.
GA94 (2014). *Überlegungen II–VI*.
   (2016) *Ponderings II–VI*, Bloomington: Indiana University Press.
GA95 (2014). *Überlegungen VII–XI*.
   (2017) *Ponderings VII–XI*, Bloomington: Indiana University Press.
GA96 (2014). *Überlegungen XII–XV*.
   (2017) *Ponderings XII–XV*, Bloomington: Indiana University Press.
GA97 (2015). *Anmerkungen I–V*.
GA98 (2018). *Anmerkungen VI–IX*.
GA99 (2019). *Vier Hefte I und II*.
GA100 (2020). *Vigiliae und Notturno*.
   (2025) *Vigils and Nocturne*, Bloomington: Indiana University Press.
GA101 (2020). *Winke I, II*.
GA102 (2022). *Vorläufiges I–IV*.

Other Sources

Adluri, V. (2011). *Parmenides, Plato, and Mortal Becoming*, London: Continuum.
Auerbach, E. (1953). *Mimesis*, Princeton, NJ: Princeton University Press.

References

Backman, J. (2015). *Complicated Presence*, Albany: State University of New York.
Backman, J., Carman, T., Dahlstrom, D., Harman, G., and Marder, M. (2019). Symposium: Beyond presence? *Gatherings*, 9, 145–74.
Berger, L. (2023). *The Politics of Attention and the Promise of Mindfulness*, Lanham, MD: Rowman & Littlefield.
Blattner, W. (1999). *Heidegger's Temporal Idealism*, Cambridge: Cambridge University Press.
Braver, L. (2012). *Groundless Grounds*, Cambridge, MA: MIT Press.
Braver, L. (2014). *Heidegger*, Cambridge: Polity.
Braver, L., ed. (2015). *Division III of Heidegger's "Being and Time,"* Cambridge, MA: MIT Press.
Capobianco, R. (2021). Presencing (*Anwesen*). In M. Wrathall, ed., *The Cambridge Heidegger Lexicon*, Cambridge: Cambridge University Press, pp. 603–5.
Capobianco, R. (2022). *Heidegger's Being*, Toronto: University of Toronto Press.
Carman, T. (1995). Heidegger's concept of presence. *Inquiry*, 38(4), 431–53.
Dastur, F. (2014). Time, event and presence in the late Heidegger. *Continental Philosophy Review*, 47, 399–421.
Derrida, J. (2016). *Heidegger*, Chicago: University of Chicago Press.
Dreyfus, H. (1991). *Being-in-the-World*, Cambridge, MA: MIT Press.
Gonzalez, F. (2006). Whose metaphysics of presence? *Southern Journal of Philosophy*, 44, 533–68.
Gonzalez, F. (2019). Shattering presence. *Journal of the History of Philosophy*, 57(2), 313–38.
Hartog, F. (2015). *Regimes of Historicity*, New York: Columbia University Press.
Hernández, J. P. (2011). How presencing (*Anwesen*) became Heidegger's concept of being. *Universitas Philosophica*, 57, 213–40.
Hughes, E., and Stendera, M. (2024). *Heidegger's Alternative History of Time*, New York: Routledge.
Husserl, E. (1964). *The Phenomenology of Internal Time-Consciousness*, Bloomington: Indiana University Press.
Jay, M. (1993). *Downcast Eyes*, Berkeley: University of California Press.
Jungk, R. (1958). *Brighter than a Thousand Suns*, New York: Harcourt.
Kirkland, S. (2023). *Heidegger and the Destruction of Aristotle*, Evanston, IL: Northwestern University Press.
Malpas, J. (2008). *Heidegger's Topology*, Cambridge, MA: MIT Press.

References

Marx, W. (1971). *Heidegger and the Tradition*, Evanston, IL: Northwestern University Press.

McNeill, W. (2020). *The Fate of Phenomenology*, Lanham, MD: Rowman & Littlefield.

Mitchell, A. (2015). *The Fourfold*, Evanston, IL: Northwestern University Press.

Nietzsche, F. (1962). *Philosophy in the Tragic Age of the Greeks*, Washington, DC: Regnery.

Nietzsche, F. (1980). *On the Advantage and Disadvantage of History for Life*, Indianapolis, IN: Hackett.

Nietzsche, F. (1997). *Twilight of the Idols*, Indianapolis, IN: Hackett.

Noë, A. (2012). *Varieties of Presence*, Cambridge, MA: Harvard University Press.

Olafson, F. (1996). Heidegger on presence: A reply. *Inquiry*, 39(3–4), 421–26.

Pippin, R. (2024). *The Culmination*, Chicago: University of Chicago Press.

Polt, R. (2006). *The Emergency of Being*, Ithaca, NY: Cornell University Press.

Polt, R. (2011). Meaning, excess, and event. *Gatherings: The Heidegger Circle Annual*, 1, 26–53.

Polt, R. (2018). Eidetic eros and the liquidation of the real. In R. Polt and J. Wittrock, eds., *The Task of Philosophy in the Anthropocene*, London: Rowman & Littlefield, pp. 63–83.

Polt, R. (2019). *Time and Trauma: Thinking through Heidegger in the Thirties*, London: Rowman & Littlefield.

Polt, R. (2020). A running leap into the there. *Graduate Faculty Philosophy Journal*, 41(1), 55–71.

Rohland, R. A. (2023). *Carpe Diem*, Cambridge: Cambridge University Press.

Rutherford, I. (2001). *Pindar's "Paeans,"* Oxford: Oxford University Press.

Sallis, J. (1984). Heidegger/Derrida – presence. *Journal of Philosophy*, 81(10), 594–601.

Schürmann, R. (1987). *Heidegger on Being and Acting*, Bloomington: Indiana University Press.

Sheehan, T. (2014). *Making Sense of Heidegger*, London: Rowman & Litttlefield.

Sinn, D. (1991). *Ereignis und Nirwana*, Bonn: Bouvier.

Tamm, M., and Olivier, L., eds. (2019). *Rethinking Historical Time*, London: Bloomsbury.

Wiener, N. (1948). *Cybernetics*, New York: Wiley.

Young, J. (2002). *Heidegger's Later Philosophy*, Cambridge: Cambridge University Press.

Zarader, M. (2006). *The Unthought Debt*, Stanford, CA: Stanford University Press.

Cambridge Elements

The Philosophy of Martin Heidegger

Series Editors
Filippo Casati
Lehigh University

Filippo Casati is an Assistant Professor at Lehigh University. He has published an array of articles in such venues as *The British Journal for the History of Philosophy, Synthese, Logique et Analyse, Philosophia, Philosophy Compass* and *The European Journal of Philosophy*. He is the author of *Heidegger and the Contradiction of Being* (Routledge) and, with Daniel O. Dahlstrom, he edited *Heidegger on Logic* (Cambridge University Press).

Daniel O. Dahlstrom
Boston University

Daniel O. Dahlstrom, John R. Silber Professor of Philosophy at Boston University, has edited twenty volumes, translated Mendelssohn, Schiller, Hegel, Husserl, Heidegger, and Landmann-Kalischer, and authored *Heidegger's Concept of Truth* (2001), *The Heidegger Dictionary* (2013; second extensively expanded edition, 2023), *Identity, Authenticity, and Humility* (2017) and over 185 essays, principally on 18th-20th century German philosophy. With Filippo Casati, he edited *Heidegger on Logic* (Cambridge University Press).

About the Series

A continual source of inspiration and controversy, the work of Martin Heidegger challenges thinkers across traditions and has opened up previously unexplored dimensions of Western thinking. The Elements in this series critically examine the continuing impact and promise of a thinker who transformed early twentieth-century phenomenology, spawned existentialism, gave new life to hermeneutics, celebrated the truthfulness of art and poetry, uncovered the hidden meaning of language and being, warned of "forgetting" being, and exposed the ominously deep roots of the essence of modern technology in Western metaphysics. Concise and structured overviews of Heidegger's philosophy offer original and clarifying approaches to the major themes of Heidegger's work, with fresh and provocative perspectives on its significance for contemporary thinking and existence.

Cambridge Elements ≡

The Philosophy of Martin Heidegger

Elements in the Series

Heidegger on Being Affected
Katherine Withy

Heidegger on Eastern/Asian Thought
Lin Ma

Heidegger on Thinking
Lee Braver

Heidegger's Concept of Science
Paul Goldberg

Heidegger on Poetic Thinking
Charles Bambach

Heidegger on Religion
Benjamin D. Crowe

Heidegger and Kierkegaard
George Pattison

Heidegger on Technology's Danger and Promise in the Age of AI
Iain D. Thomson

Heidegger On Presence
Richard Polt

A full series listing is available at: www.cambridge.org/EPMH

For EU product safety concerns, contact us at Calle de José Abascal, 56–1°, 28003 Madrid, Spain or eugpsr@cambridge.org.

www.ingramcontent.com/pod-product-compliance
Lightning Source LLC
LaVergne TN
LVHW020351260326
834688LV00045B/1669